DATE DUE

The Minnesota Community

Lowry Nelson ━━━━━━━━━━━━━━━━ ☙

The Minnesota Community

COUNTRY AND TOWN IN TRANSITION

The University of Minnesota Press, Minneapolis

Preface

THIS book is about Minnesota's people — those of yesterday and to-day, those who laid foundations and those who built the superstructures of community life. It is about the institutions the people established and the influences which helped or impeded their efforts.

The focus is upon Minnesota's rural people, but they are seen in the context of the Great Society. Although all the people were rural in the beginning, cities emerged early in the state's history and grew rapidly. The completely rural society was short-lived as the urban-industrial world soon appeared and gradually emerged into predominance. Some of the reasons for this steady and insistent transition in the Minnesota community are presented in this volume.

The emphasis is on social change, the major but little understood influence which shapes the lives of men. The book makes no pretense of contributing to the fundamental nature of change, but does reveal some measurements of it: it shows some of the many trails we have traveled in a century of time. Trends in some aspects of the state's social development can be measured and some of these trends are charted here.

The state as a unit for study of social change offers some advantages. It is large enough to comprise the major segments of life — farm, village, city — yet small enough that the data are manageable; social processes are thus easier to discern. By and large, sociologists have focused their attention upon the local community, and for purposes of intensive analysis this becomes necessary. But the state may also be viewed as a community for

v

purposes of examining the large aspects of change. Even the nation must be taken as the unit of analysis for certain purposes.

The state of Minnesota offers special advantages for the study of social change. It contains a large farm population, numerous small rural trade centers with fewer than 2,500 people; many small cities between these, and the two metropolitan areas of the Twin Cities and Duluth. It is a fair sample of the nation itself: its agriculture and industry are well diversified and it is especially well adapted for the study of rural-urban integration, one of the processes emphasized herein.

This small book, really an expanded essay, grows out of twenty-one years of experience in investigating rural community life at the University of Minnesota. Much more research than can be reported here has been done during this time and during the services of my predecessors: Carle C. Zimmerman, who served as the first rural sociologist on the Agricultural Experiment Station staff from 1925 to 1930 before leaving for his present position at Harvard University; and the late Robert W. Murchie, who served from 1931 to 1937.

To attempt to include a comprehensive review of this research would, however, prove unduly tiring to the reader and would make this book too long. Most of the research results have been reported in bulletins and other publications of the University of Minnesota Agricultural Experiment Station and in professional journals, and are thus available in libraries for anyone who might wish to consult them.

In the course of the years during which I have served at the University of Minnesota, I have enjoyed and profited greatly from the stimulation of the intellectual environment created by colleagues and students. A number of graduate students have served as research assistants and have contributed to the growing fund of information about rural life of the state. Most of them have received advanced degrees, and their theses have become part of the literature of rural sociology.

Colleagues in Rural Sociology to whom I owe a great debt for their intellectual stimulation and their congenial association are Afif I. Tannous, 1940–1942, now with the Foreign Agricultural Service, United States Department of Agriculture; Frank D. Alexander, 1946–1948, now associate professor in the Extension Service, Cornell University; Douglas G. Marshall, 1946–1952, now professor of rural sociology at the University of Wisconsin; Charles E. Ramsey, 1951–1953, now associate professor of rural sociology at Cornell University; Roy G. Francis, Marvin J. Taves,

George A. Donohue, and Charles W. Martin, all present members of the staff.

For assistance with the manuscript at various stages my thanks to Miss Marian Cure, Mrs. Agnes Kohan, Miss Clarice Olien, Miss Dawn Carnahan, and my wife, Florence. A special debt of gratitude I owe to Miss Marcia Strout of the University of Minnesota Press for painstaking and intelligent editing of the manuscript. These and many more not mentioned by name have had a part in this enterprise and I remember them with deep gratitude. Of course, the shortcomings of the work are of my own making.

LOWRY NELSON

Contents

I UNDER ALL, THE LAND   3

II THE PEOPLE CAME   18

III OF KINDREDS, TONGUES, AND PEOPLES   39

IV FAMILIES OLD AND NEW   54

V THE REACH AND THE GRASP   70

VI THERE SHALL BE EDUCATION IN THE LAND   83

VII GOVERNMENT FOR THE PEOPLE   99

VIII THE CHURCHES: FROM CABIN TO CATHEDRAL   114

IX THE CUTOVER: OUR RURAL PROBLEM AREA   126

X THE FUTURE WILL BE DIFFERENT   147

BIBLIOGRAPHY   167

APPENDIX: POPULATION TABLES   169

INDEX   172

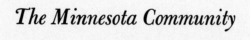

The Minnesota Community

1 Under All, the Land

A REMARKABLE and sobering fact about our planet is that all forms of life, including man, depend upon a thin layer of topsoil often no more than a few inches deep. Within this marvelous association of organisms and minerals, and by virtue of the miracle of photosynthesis through which sunlight gives its life-giving power, all the food that sustains life in any form is produced. Because man has a superior intelligence, he has been able to cooperate with forces of nature in greatly accelerating the earth's productivity.

Most of this acceleration has taken place within the comparatively recent past. Although man in some form has been on the planet for many thousands of years, his mastery over nature came slowly. The invention of agriculture is fairly recent, say around twenty thousand years ago. Before that, it was impossible for human beings to establish permanent abodes; they were either nomadic herdsmen following their flocks from summer to winter pastures and back, or, in the tropics, wanderers ever moving their villages from an exhausted area to a new one.

At the dawn of the period when men began to keep records of their activities, agriculture was well developed in the Mesopotamian and Mediterranean basins, and possibly in many other parts of Europe and Asia. By the time settlement of the New World by people of European descent began, the arts of producing plants and animals had reached a relatively high state. When the nineteenth century opened, most of the basic breeds of livestock known today had already been developed, chiefly in the

3

British Isles; and much progress had been made in crop culture. But most of the mechanical inventions that were to release so much new power for agriculture were yet to come. The plow that broke the plains, for example, came into being around the time of the Civil War. And, of course, the application of the internal combustion engine to agriculture came during the present century.

There Was a Time for Discoveries [1]

More than a century elapsed after Columbus's discovery of America before a permanent settlement of Europeans was established at Plymouth. Three or four decades after this, daring French explorers — Radisson and Groseilliers — penetrated to the interior of the continent and are generally considered to be the first white men to see any part of the area now known as Minnesota. Following them came others from New France — traders, fur-gatherers, missionaries: Nicolet, Marquette, Hennepin, Du Lhut, and others. "The land was here before the people came."

Claims to the territory by European powers shifted from one to another up to 1800. In 1763, by the Treaty of Paris, the area east of the Mississippi was ceded by France to England, that west of the river having been given by France to Spain the previous year. The success of the American Revolution wrested control of the territory east of the Mississippi from England. Napoleon reclaimed for France the territory west of the Mississippi in 1800, but in 1803 he negotiated with President Thomas Jefferson its sale to the United States. This brought all of the area now included in Minnesota into the hands of the United States, as far as the claims of peoples of European origin were concerned. There remained to be settled those of the various Indian tribes, which ultimately were successfully negotiated.

When the first settlers came to what is now Minnesota, they truly came to a virgin land. Although it had been inhabited from time immemorial and considerable populations had found their sustenance in the natural yields of its woods and streams, it was largely unexploited agriculturally. The original inhabitants knew nothing of agriculture as the Europeans

---

[1] "There was a time for discoveries — / For the headlands looming above in the / First light and the surf and the / Crying of gulls: for the curve of the / Coast north into secrecy.// That time is past./ The last lands have been peopled./ The oceans are known now." From "Voyage West," Archibald MacLeish, *Actfive and Other Poems* (New York: Random House, 1948). By permission of the author and the publisher.

4

practiced it. As soon as treaties could be arranged between the natives and the United States government to quiet the Indians' claims, the newcomers from Europe began to till the soil and to introduce their advanced system of agriculture.

In the early 1820's — just two centuries after the landing of the Pilgrims — the settlement of Minnesota by white immigrants from the adjacent Canadian areas was well under way. In 1821, for example, five families from Lord Selkirk's colony near the present Winnipeg settled near Fort Snelling, which had been constructed in 1819. By 1835 about five hundred persons had arrived at Fort Snelling from the Red River settlements. Since Fort Snelling was a military reservation, the settlers in 1837 were required to move to what is now St. Paul, then known as Pig's Eye.

Treaties with Indians in 1837 opened to white settlement the territory between the St. Croix and the Mississippi Rivers north to the mouth of the Crow Wing River. In this year Duluth, Crow Wing and St. Croix were established; in 1839, Marine–on–St. Croix and in 1843, Stillwater. The latter two towns were settled mostly by New Englanders, who were familiar with lumbering. They soon established mills, and lumbering became the basic industry of this area.

After the first land sale in 1848, immigration flowed in from the East, mainly New York, Pennsylvania, and the New England states. Minnesota Territory was established by Congress in 1849. Besides what is now the state of Minnesota, the territory encompassed much of the area now included in North and South Dakota.

The Land Is Mine, All Mine [2]

The newcomers to Minnesota obtained land under the various laws in effect at the time of arrival. Those who came before the Homestead Act of 1862 had to purchase for cash and usually at the minimum price of $1.25 an acre. The first land office was opened at St. Croix Falls, Wisconsin, in 1847 and made the first sales of land in the territory. At the first public sale on August 14, 1848, 3,326 acres were sold at $1.25 an acre. Townsites for Stillwater, St. Paul, and St. Anthony were also en-

[2] "When I am plowing I can shut my eyes and smell the dear land under me and say it is mine, mine, all mine. No one can take it away. I am king as you said. . . ." From a letter to his mother by a settler from East Frisia published in E. T. Hiller, Faye E. Corner, and Wendell L. East, "Rural Community Types," *University of Illinois Studies in the Social Sciences*, Vol. XVI, No. 4, p. 27.

tered at the St. Croix Falls office.[3] Then the land office was moved to Stillwater, and the first public sale of lands took place there in October, 1849.

A settler who occupied land before it was surveyed was called a squatter, and until the Pre-emption Act of 1841 was passed, he ran the risk of having someone else buy his claim who was able and willing to pay more than the settler himself. The Pre-emption Act gave the settler a prior right to buy the land on which he had made improvements and established his home. Some were able to get military bounty warrants, issued originally to veterans of past wars, which entitled them to a homestead on the public domain. The veteran who did not wish to execute his warrant could sell it to a broker, who in turn would sell it to a land speculator, or to a bona fide settler, usually for much less than $1.25 an acre.

After 1862, settlers could homestead their claims, and, by satisfying the requirements of the law regarding residence on the claim and making certain improvements, could obtain title after five years. Also in 1862, Congress passed the Morrill Act, which provided for the establishment of an agricultural and mechanical college in each of the states and authorized grants of land on the public domain as an endowment. These grants amounted to something like a hundred thousand acres per state. For those states that contained no public domain, such as the New England states, land scrip was issued which could be used to get land on the public domain in any state where such unappropriated lands existed.

The federal government made various grants to Minnesota when it became a state in 1858. In addition to the land grant of the agricultural and mechanical college, there was a similar grant for the state university. Certain swamp lands were also turned over to the state, and sections 16 and 36 of each township were reserved for the support of public schools. Settlers therefore purchased such lands directly from the state and the funds went into a permanent endowment for the support of education.

Grants of land to encourage railroad construction, which the railroads later "colonized," were also made by the federal government. Some of the ways in which lands were alienated from the public domain up to around 1880 are shown in the accompanying tabulation.[4]

[3] Merrill E. Jarchow, *The Earth Brought Forth*, (St. Paul: Minnesota Historical Society, 1949) p. 25.
[4] *Ibid.*, p. 78.

Acres

Cash sales and warrants...............	8,920,285
Homestead and Timber Culture acts......	5,829,043
School lands........................	2,969,990
Internal Improvement grant............	500,000
Railroad grants......................	7,621,132
Agricultural college and university........	1,126,457
Swamp lands........................	1,361,125
Other	277,907
Total	28,605,939

After the acquisition of a patent from the federal government, many farm families found themselves faced with the need for more capital. This was usually secured, in the early periods, by mortgaging the land to private lenders. After the creation of the Federal Land Banks in 1916, farmers were able to borrow funds at relatively low rates of interest with payments spread over thirty-three years. The private lenders had not only charged higher rates of interest but were seldom willing or able to lend money for more than ten years.

How the Land Was Divided

Even though the land was "open" in 1850, that year marked but the beginning of the acquisition of land for farms, for the census-takers found in 1850 only 157 farms in Minnesota. From then on the increase was rapid and steady up to 1900 when there were 154,659 farms enclosing 26,248,498 acres. There was virtually no increase up to 1910, but a spurt to 178,478 by 1920 reflected the expansion for food production during World War I. The number of farms, acreage, and average size is shown in Table 1.

The number of farms and the acreage seemed to reach a plateau around 1920. The expansion during World War I did not lose momentum until the early 1920's, when the postwar depression came. But the depression of the 1930's resulted in another increase, not because there was still a great demand for farm products, for there was already a depressing surplus, but rather because there was nothing else for people to do. The people from farms who would ordinarily have left for jobs in industry could not get out; the jobs did not exist. So when the census-taker came around in 1935, he found a great many more cultivated tracts which met the census definition of a farm. Since that year, the decline in

7

farms has been continuous with a rather precipitate drop between 1930 and 1954. The average acreage per farm increased steadily from 1860 to 1910, after which it declined up to 1925, when it began a rise that has become more marked with each new decade.

But there are small, medium, and large farms. Averages conceal important facts, despite their convenience as summarizing devices. The

Table 1. Number of Farms, Total Acreage, and Average
Acreage per Farm, 1850–1955

Year	No. of Farms	Acreage	Average Acreage per Farm
1850............	157	28,881	183.9
1860............	18,024	2,711,968	149.2
1870............	46,500	6,483,828	139.4
1880............	92,386	13,403,019	145.1
1890............	116,851	18,663,645	159.7
1900............	154,659	26,248,498	169.7
1910............	156,137	27,675,823	177.3
1920............	178,478	30,221,758	169.3
1925............	188,231	30,059,137	159.7
1930............	185,255	30,913,367	166.9
1935............	203,302	32,817,011	161.4
1940............	197,351	32,606,962	165.2
1945............	188,952	33,139,997	175.4
1950............	179,101	32,883,165	183.6
1955............	165,225	32,284,539	195.4

typical farm in our history has been the old homestead of nostalgic recollection. This was 160 acres, and it is interesting to note that the average acreage per farm has varied little from that size. In 1954 there were more farms in Minnesota from 140 to 179 acres — which would include the homestead — than in any other size group: 35,864 in all. However, they constituted less than a fifth of all farms. There were almost twice as many that were smaller than 140 acres, and about twice as many that were larger.

It is of importance to note which sizes of farms have been increasing and which decreasing in recent years. Figure 1 shows what has been happening. Briefly, farms smaller than 180 acres have declined in number between 1940 and 1954; larger ones have proliferated. The percentage of those of 1,000 acres or more has increased more than any, but there still were only 725 in the entire state in this size group in 1954. There

8

was a significant number — 30,842 — in the size group from 260 to 499 acres. Next to the homestead group mentioned above this size of farm is the most numerous.

These figures may give rise to the fear that the large farm is going to crowd out the small ones, and nobody can say at this writing that the

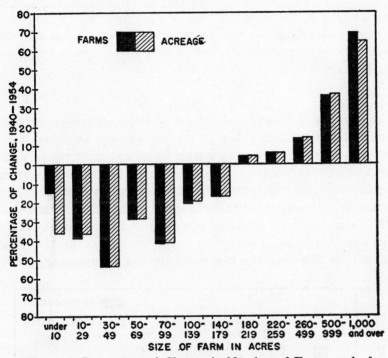

Figure 1. Percentage of Change in Number of Farms and of Acreage in Farms in Minnesota by Size of Farm from 1940 to 1954

fear is not justified. Some people in fact do not fear such a trend; they chalk it up to "progress," and progress is something not to be interfered with. But there are always some impediments to such a complete modification in our rural way of life. Not all farm operators are able to operate larger units than they now have. Many are not interested in trying to do so even though they might be competent. And there are all the various motivations that influence people in a free society to make decisions. As far as the family farm is concerned, it cannot be validly said that increasing the size of a farm makes it something else. Mechanization and new methods of management make a very large farm a family farm still. Yet we do seem to be witnessing an increasing concentration of ownership of land. What the outcome will be it is impossible now to predict.

Part-owner farms increased from 19 to 22 per cent in the period from 1950 to 1954. This represents a tendency by farm owners to try to increase the size of their farms by renting from neighbors who for one reason or another do not wish to sell — or perhaps the operator does not wish to buy. Part-owners are usually operators of larger farms, on the average, than either owners or tenants.

Tenancy

The hazards of farming being what they are, many farmers lost their land in the various depressions of the past century. Droughts, severe outbreaks of insect pests, unseasonable frosts, and other natural disasters have also contributed to farmers' financial failure. Along with inheritance laws, these and other factors have resulted in a decline in farm ownership and a corresponding rise in tenancy. Figure 2 shows that since 1935 (when tenancy reached its high point of 34 per cent) there has been a gradual decline in the rate of tenancy from 34 per cent to 19 per cent in 1954. The proportion of owned farms has correspondingly risen.

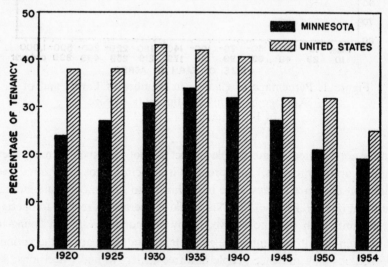

Figure 2. Comparative Trends in Farm Tenancy in Minnesota
and in the United States from 1920 to 1954

While farm ownership has been a traditional objective of the farm people of the United States and was undoubtedly a dominant purpose of the early Minnesota settlers, the attainment of the goal is not always possible, and very seldom easy. Farm ownership is ordinarily associated in the public mind with stability of occupancy and with high participation in the affairs of the community. This is not always the case for a number of reasons. First of all, we have noted that the high ownership rates in Minnesota are in the northern forested area where land tends to be cheap and productivity low. And this is precisely the area where mobility is highest. In the area of greatest productivity in the southern part of the state, tenancy is high and mobility low. In the minds of many people, also, tenancy is associated with poor land. On the contrary, there can be tenancy only on the better land, for in order for tenancy to exist a farm must be able to support the owning family as well as the tenant. Moreover, in the most productive parts of the state, the capital required for farm ownership and operation is so great that many operators are unable to obtain it immediately. Many young men just beginning their careers as farmers undertake to rent for a time until they are able to buy the farm.

By contrast, in the northern forested area of the state, land is less productive on the whole, and may often be purchased at a very low cost. Since this land generally is not able to support more than one family, the tenancy rate is very low. Tenancy, it should be noted here, is not to be regarded as an evil. Indeed it is often the only way young men can get started in farming. Many tenants are related to the owners — sons, sons-in-law, or other relatives. It often happens that a farmer decides to retire from operation of the farm and allows one of the sons or a son-in-law to take over the active management. Since there are other heirs to the property, the son operates the farm on a lease. Eventually he may buy the rights of the other heirs and obtain full ownership.

Social significance of tenancy. Tenancy in Minnesota does not carry with it the lower social status which is common in, say, some of the southern states. Tenants are frequently related to the owner, and are simply at one stage in their advance toward ultimate ownership. Again, some tenants prefer to remain tenants as long as they are assured of stable occupancy of the farm, rather than assume the risks of ownership. Such tenants as these do not differ significantly from owners in their partici-

11

pation in the community. They belong to the farm organizations and cooperatives and take part in agricultural extension work. Their children, as readily as those of owners, join 4-H clubs and other community youth groups.

Age and tenancy. Yet some differences may arise between the behavior of tenants and owners which are not the result of tenancy directly but rather of secondary factors associated with it. One of these is the age of the operator. Tenants are younger on the average than owners. It will be seen from Figure 3 that farm operators are younger in southwestern Minnesota in precisely the area with highest tenancy, and conversely that the oldest operators are in northeastern Minnesota where the tenancy rate is lowest. Indeed, rankings of the counties on average age of operators and on the percentage of tenancy are almost identical, show an almost perfect inverse correlation (rho = $-.97$). The younger the operators, the higher the rate of tenancy. Differences in age may result in differences in community participation and attitudes. Tenancy is only indirectly involved and it in turn is the consequence of the operation of other factors.

Part-Time Farming

A phenomenon of growing importance is the tendency for farmers to be employed part time off the farm. It is estimated that in the United States in 1957 one third of all income of farm people was derived from nonfarm sources. Part-time farmers are of many kinds. There are some, semi-retired and living on the outskirts of cities, who supplement income from nonfarm employment, or from pensions, by operating a small acreage. Others are technically operators of large farms, who, because of mechanization, are able to leave the work on the farm to grown children or even to the wife, while they do full-time jobs in town or city. Some work on highways, in mines or forests, or in other enterprises. In some cases, adult children may be employed off the farm but continue to live at home. The percentage of Minnesota farmers working one hundred days or more off their farms has increased from 6.5 per cent in 1930 to 12.6 per cent in 1950, to 15 per cent in 1954. The percentages vary with the type of farming and other factors, from a high of over 50 per cent in some counties of northeastern Minnesota to 2 per cent in Nobles County in southwestern Minnesota. In general, the rate is high in the north and low in the south. Opportunities for employment off the farm

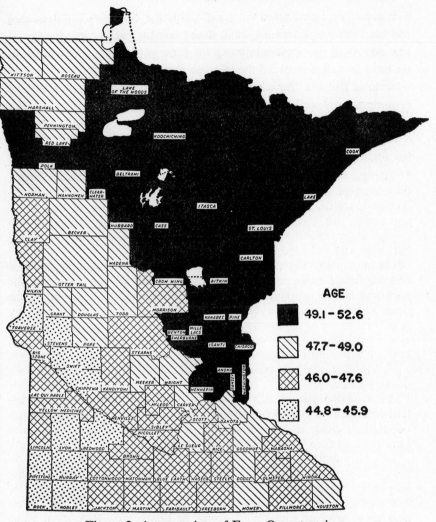

AGE

■ 49.1 – 52.6

▨ 47.7 – 49.0

▧ 46.0 – 47.6

⠿ 44.8 – 45.9

Figure 3. Average Age of Farm Operators in
Minnesota in 1954

have something to do with the rate, and account in part for the high rate
in the northeast, where work is available in mines and forests and industries based upon them. On the other hand, the grain and livestock
farming of the southwest provides full employment, or at least adequate
income, so that off-farm work either cannot be undertaken or is not
needed by the family.

13

THE MINNESOTA COMMUNITY

What of part-time farming? As of the late 1950's very little research has been done to determine what, if any, are the social consequences of this important development among the farm population. The census, as we have seen, has recorded the increase in work off the farm by the farm operators. But the characteristics of those who engage in this kind of farming are not well known.

In a 1955 study of 167 part- and full-time farm operators near the Twin Cities, George A. Donohue drew the following conclusions from his findings:

The part-time farmer differs significantly from the full-time farmer on a number of objective characteristics such as age, education, socio-economic status, farm ownership, type of off-farm work, marital status and family size. Even though these differences exist they do not appear to have an appreciable effect in creating different attitude patterns among part-time and full-time farmers.

On the basis of the absence of significant differences among part-time and full-time farmers with respect to social attitudes, the thesis that the part-time farmer is a cultural hybrid and contributes to instability in the rural structure appears questionable. A fruitful avenue for further research might be to determine the degree to which the part-time farmer's urban participation tends to be nominal or passive, and thus results in little influence on his attitudes and behaviors outside of the immediate work situation. His reference group appears to be mainly that of the full-time operator.

A factor that may account for lack of significant differences is the extent to which part-time farmers are recruited from the full-time farm population, either as sons of farmers on the brink of retirement, who have reduced their scale of operations and who engaged in off-farm work in order to supplement their small farm incomes. The individual of urban background without farming experience engaging in part-time farming was an extremely rare occurrence.

Plausibly, persons engaging in part-time farming (e.g., "hobby" farmers) may have, in addition to economic motivation, a personal value orientation in accord with the value orientation of full-time farmers and the rural social structure, thus contributing to homogeneity rather than heterogeneity.[5]

Another study also found little difference in attitudes between part-time and other farmers. Of a sample of 575 full and part-time farmers living in the thirteen counties of the northern forested area, designated

[5] George A. Donohue, "Socio-Economic Characteristics of Part-time and Full-time Farmers in the Twin-Cities Area," *Farm Economics*, Vol. 39, No. 4 (November, 1957), pp. 984–992.

14

a low-income farm area, questions were asked regarding government price-support programs. The questions were:

1. Do you think government price support programs have helped you in any way?
2. Have they hurt you?
3. With your experience in farming, what do you think should be done about price support programs? (or which plan do you think best?)
4. How important do you think a sound agricultural program is to keeping city and town people prosperous?

The conclusion was that "whether or not the operator was a full-time or part-time operator did not make any significant difference in the type of support program he preferred." [6]

Types of Farming Areas

Differences in climate, soil, and historical and cultural circumstances have given rise to differences in the crops and livestock which farmers produce. The various combinations of crops and animals are referred to as types of farming. For example, in some portions of the state the production of corn and livestock is dominant; in others, dairying; in others, grain and potatoes; and so on. The Department of Agricultural Economics of the Institute of Agriculture, University of Minnesota, has distinguished nine such areas (see Figure 4), the ninth consisting of Ramsey and Hennepin Counties in which the Twin Cities are located. Each area includes counties which are alike in the type of farming done in them; that is, homogeneity is the principle governing the determination of the areas. This grouping according to crop and livestock combinations does not mean that the same combinations do not occur in other counties, but merely that they are more conspicuous or dominant in a particular area than in others. For example, to call one area (southwestern Minnesota) part of the Corn Belt does not mean that it is the only place corn is grown; corn is grown in every other area as well, but it is not so important in some counties.

Climates and soil may remain the same in these areas, but the level of technology changes. This change in turn makes it possible to grow different crops in areas once thought to be suited only for those originally

[6] George A. Donohue and Lowry Nelson, "What Do Cutover Area Farmers Think about Price Supports?," *Minnesota Farm and Home Science*, Vol. 15, No. 2 (February, 1958), pp. 12–13.

introduced. For instance, wheat, once so important in the Red River Valley, has become a minor product there and has given way to such crops as sugarbeets and potatoes. Again, in examining the records of farms of southeastern Minnesota from 1928 to 1952, Pond and Nodland noted a decrease in the proportion of tillable land devoted to small grains and canning-peas, and increases in the proportions in corn, soybeans, and other cultivated crops, as well as an increase in the land in hay;

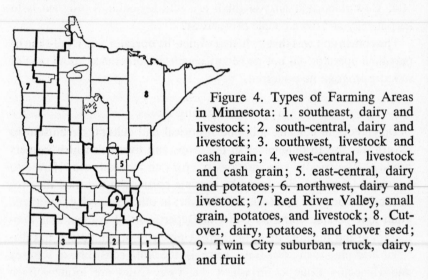

Figure 4. Types of Farming Areas in Minnesota: 1. southeast, dairy and livestock; 2. south-central, dairy and livestock; 3. southwest, livestock and cash grain; 4. west-central, livestock and cash grain; 5. east-central, dairy and potatoes; 6. northwest, dairy and livestock; 7. Red River Valley, small grain, potatoes, and livestock; 8. Cutover, dairy, potatoes, and clover seed; 9. Twin City suburban, truck, dairy, and fruit

heads of livestock per hundred acres showed a marked increase.[7] Such changes come about when technical agricultural research finds ways to develop crops and animals adapted to particular climatic and soil conditions. Market conditions also affect farming systems: food habits change, creating greater demand for some foods and less for others. For example, the per-capita consumption of wheat and potatoes has been declining for many years, while the consumption of green and yellow vegetables, fruits, and dairy products has been rising. These changes come gradually, however, and there is a certain degree of stability in the areas.

Social characteristics. The percentage of the population of the area that is rural farm, the number of children under 5 per 1,000 farm women aged 15 to 49, the percentage of the total population under 15, males

[7] George A. Pond and Truman R. Nodland, *The Changing Picture of Farming in Southeastern Minnesota*, Minnesota Agricultural Experiment Station Bulletin 446 (January 1958), p. 8.

per 100 females — all these vary among the types of farming areas. For example, area 6 (see Figure 4) with 47 per cent of its population rural farm, had 597 children under 5 for every 1,000 women 15–49; comparable figures for area 3 with 21 per cent rural farm was 452. Area 6 had 131 males per 100 females compared with 146 for area 3. Other areas fall between these extremes. In later chapters, including those dealing with education and religion, additional differences among the areas will be noted, which further demonstrate that type of farming areas are clearly cultural areas.

The natural and cultural factors which have formed the basis for the demarcation of regions of the state — soil, climate, and the level of technical arts, plus the ethnic backgrounds of the people — also make for differences in other than economic behavior. In other words, the agricultural regions are also cultural regions, or to put it simply, *agriculture is culture*. And although changes are certain to come that will alter the boundaries of these areas, some differences will most likely always persist among them. Indeed, the differences may become more clearly marked as the trend toward specialization in agriculture continues. Dairying may become more highly concentrated in certain areas; the same can be said of poultry production, livestock feeding, and so on. It is not easy to foresee what will happen with the continued emphasis on technical agricultural research on the one hand, and the drive toward even more efficient farm organization on the other.

Robert Frost has observed, "The land was here before the people came." He was thinking of Europeans, but it would have been equally true to say this of the American Indians. There was the "time for discoveries" as Archibald MacLeish put it, but "the people came" rapidly on the heels of the voyageurs, the discoverers. In the short time — as history goes — of a hundred years, MacLeish can truly say "The last lands have been peopled." The people of Minnesota are the subject of the next chapter.[8]

[8] The story of the development of Minnesota from its beginning is told in a very readable book by T. C. Blegen, *The Land Lies Open* (Minneapolis: University of Minnesota Press, 1949).

II The People Came

A HUNDRED years is but a moment in historical time, but in terms of recent human experience the last century is a period of remarkable changes. I emphasize *recent* because it probably required several hundred thousand years for man to increase his numbers to the first billion, about a century ago. Since then he has more than doubled his numbers.[1]

A little more than four and a half centuries ago, the great Western Hemisphere was not even known to exist by Europeans and Asians. It was peopled by human beings, but very sparsely. The indigenous peoples knew little of agriculture and could not support large numbers from the natural, unaided resources of the land. Some of them had developed a limited agriculture based on corn, a crop unknown in Europe. European immigrants brought to the New World more highly developed arts of animal and plant production, adopted the strange plant and its method of cultivation and use from the Indians, and then greatly improved corn and the methods of growing it.

One of the most important changes during the hundred-plus years since the Europeans began to settle the land of Minnesota is the sheer increase in population. It is important because an increase in numbers of people brings many modifications in social organization. Perhaps the most im-

[1] Much of the data in this chapter is derived from the following bulletins of the Minnesota Agricultural Experiment Station: Lowry Nelson, Charles E. Ramsey, and Jacob Toews, *A Century of Population Growth*, Bulletin 423; Charles E. Ramsey, Allan D. Orman, and Lowry Nelson, *Migration in Minnesota 1940–50*, Bulletin 422. Earlier bulletins dealing with population were R. W. Murchie and M. E. Jarchow, *Population Trends in Minnesota*, Bulletin 327 (May, 1936), and Lowry Nelson and Hazel Clampitt, *Population Trends in Minnesota, 1940*, Bulletin 387 (June, 1945).

portant of these is the division of labor. In any pioneer period, the necessity for survival compels men to give primary and almost exclusive attention to producing food and providing shelter. Gradually, as the crises of the first years pass and the production of the land increases, it is no longer necessary for everyone to engage in the same occupations, the growing of food and the building of houses. Specialization takes place: some become merchants, some carpenters, and some take up other trades and occupations. In Minnesota the decline in the proportion of the population engaged in farming commenced early. It has continued throughout the century, with here and there some inconsequential exceptions. The increase in population also brings increases in property values, particularly urban property. The rise of towns and cities and their disproportionate growth in relation to the farm population brings increasing complexity in social organization, in political arrangements, in educational systems, and in economic and religious institutions.

Growth of the Population

Let us take a brief look at the population growth and changes in Minnesota over a century. The growth of population from 6,077 in 1850 to 2,982,483 in 1950 and an estimated 3,418,000 in 1958 is shown in Figure 5. Also shown are the trends for rural and urban segments. Expressed as percentages of increase over the previous decade, the growth in the early years was dramatic: from 1850 to 1860 the increase was over 2,700 per cent; in the 1860's the population increased 155 per cent. Since that time the growth has continued, but at a decreasing rate. In the decade of the 1940's the increase was 6.8 per cent.

The decline in the proportionate growth has been explained by the decreasing birth rate and by drastic reductions in immigration. But these are only part of the explanation. Economic and social motives have led thousands to leave Minnesota for other states. For example, in the 1940's all but five counties lost more than they gained through migration, and 178,034 more people left the state than came into it. Then too, we must recognize that the rate of growth calculated by percentage change is affected by the size of the base population: with a base population of six thousand the addition during a decade of six thousand means 100 per cent rate of growth; but with one million as a base, an addition of another million would be necessary to make 100 per cent growth. An increase of this magnitude would be fantastic.

19

Perhaps as important as the growth of the total population is the growth of particular groups within it. The long-term trends as well as the changes in the forties indicate noticeable differences in the respective rates of growth of rural and urban areas.

Urban growth. The phenomenal growth of the total state population in the early decades also characterized the urban population. In 1850 there were no cities. In the 1860's the urban population was still less than

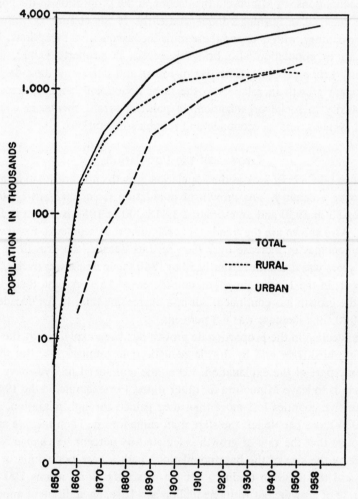

Figure 5. Population Growth in Minnesota
from 1850 to 1958

10 per cent of the total, but the proportion of the population that was urban increased steadily from then on. Although the rate of growth of the cities continued to decrease from 1870 until 1940, it increased again by 15.6 per cent from 1940 to 1950, compared with 10.5 per cent in the previous decade. It was not until 1950 that the urban population surpassed the rural (including farm and nonfarm) in Minnesota.

A change in the census definition for 1950 of the farm and nonfarm categories in the rural population should be noted: "In 1950, persons living on what might have been considered farm land were classified as nonfarm if they paid cash rent for their homes and yards only. A few persons in institutions, summer camps, "motels," and tourist camps were classified as farm residents in 1940, whereas in 1950 all such persons were classified as nonfarm." [2] For the United States as a whole the 1950 farm population would have been reported as about 9 per cent larger if the 1940 definition had been used.

The comparative growth of the urban population and of individual cities is interesting. St. Paul contained 6 per cent of the total population of Minnesota in 1860. With small variations it remained about the same proportion until the 1880's. In the 1890 census it rose to 10.2 per cent, and has continued to be about the same proportion of the total since that time: in 1950 it was 10.4 per cent.

The population of Minneapolis increased steadily as a proportion of Minnesota's population until 1930. It had only 1.5 per cent of the total in 1860, but had grown to 18.1 per cent in 1930. There was a slight decline during the thirties and forties so that in 1950 its population was 17.5 per cent of the total. Duluth's growth was similar to that of Minneapolis in long-range trends, but on a smaller scale.

The Twin Cities from the very beginning of settlement have served as regional trade centers not only for Minnesota, but for North and South Dakota and Montana to the west and for the western part of Wisconsin. For a considerable period after settlement, St. Paul was the gateway to the Red River Valley on both sides of the international border, and even to the Canadian provinces beyond it. More and more, St. Paul and Minneapolis became the transportation, milling, marketing, lumbering, financial, and manufacturing center of a vast region of the Northwest comprising thousands of square miles. Duluth became the great center

[2] United States Bureau of the Census, *Census of Population: 1950*, Part 23, p. xiv.

21

for mining and shipping with the opening of the iron mines (see Chapter IX). Thus not only are the people and resources within the boundaries of the state to be credited with the rise and growth of the urban industrial complexes of the Twin Cities and Duluth, but the contributions of an area comprising a number of states and parts of states must also be acknowledged.

The population of all other cities combined grew steadily from 1.8 per cent in 1860 to 22.5 per cent in 1950. Without exception they have made up a larger proportion of the total in each succeeding census.

Rural decline. The trend of the rural population was, of course, opposite to that of the urban. It declined steadily from 100 per cent rural in 1850 to slightly less than 50 per cent in 1950; and the decline in rate of growth, expressed as a percentage of increase over the previous decade, was much more rapid than that of the urban population.

The importance of agriculture and the rural population has undergone a vast change during the century. At the turn of the century, Minnesota was still two thirds rural; in 1940 the difference between rural and urban was negligible, although the rural still had the edge by .2 per cent; in 1950, 53.9 per cent of the population was urban (by the 1940 definition). From 1860 to 1880 more than 50 per cent of all gainfully employed workers were engaged in agriculture, compared with 30 per cent in 1940, and 22 per cent in 1950.

In the 1950 census the definition of urban was changed from that used in previous censuses. Under the old definition (1940) which is used in this chapter for all years, the urban population comprised "all persons living in incorporated places of 2,500 inhabitants or more and was classified as urban under special rules relating to population size and density." The remainder were classified as rural. The new definition, used in the 1950 census, classifies as urban "all persons living in (a) places of 2,500 inhabitants or more incorporated as cities, boroughs, towns, and villages; (b) the densely settled urban fringe, including both incorporated and unincorporated places of 2,500 inhabitants or more outside any urban fringes." [3]

The number of people living on farms was reported separately for the first time in the census of 1920. The rural nonfarm people were likewise classified separately. They consisted mainly, but not entirely, of people

[3] *Ibid.*, p. xiii.

living in places of fewer than 2,500 population. These two segments compose the rural population as defined by the census. The rural farm population, as noted earlier, has continued to decline, although the rural nonfarm group has increased. Only during the Great Depression of the 1930's has the farm population increased during any decade since 1900, and then it was but a small 2 per cent increase. The outbreak of World War II soon siphoned off the "surplus" population on farms, in answer to the call for workers in war industries and for men and women for the armed forces. During the 1940's the center of gravity of the state's population shifted at an accelerated rate toward the cities.

A direct measure of the urbanward movement is presented in the net migration of the rural population of the state. The five counties that gained through the migration — Anoka, Hennepin, Lake, Ramsey, and Washington — were all near the Twin Cities or Duluth.

Trend by areas since 1950. Using the estimates of county population made annually by the Minnesota Department of Health, it is possible to get an idea of the changes by type of farming areas since the federal census of 1950;[4] the figures for 1950 and 1957 and the magnitude and direction of change are shown in Table 2. The largest gains were for

Table 2. Change in Population by Type of Farming Area
between 1950 and 1957

Area*	Population		Gain or Loss	
	1950	1957	No.	%
1..........	314,429	359,880	45,451	14.5
2..........	401,121	449,518	48,397	12.1
3..........	190,404	203,065	12,661	6.6
4..........	189,295	196,381	7,086	3.6
5..........	155,355	182,337	27,382	17.6
6..........	203,034	202,731	−303	−0.1
7..........	89,500	96,114	6,614	7.4
8..........	407,434	443,490	36,056	8.8
9..........	1,031,911	1,173,316	141,405	13.7

*Areas are shown on Figure 4.

[4] The method of estimating county populations involves (1) determining excess of births over deaths during the year from the reports of births and deaths made to the Section of Vital Statistics of the Minnesota Department of Health, (2) estimating migration through use of school census figures supplied by the Minnesota Department of Education. The number of children in the age group 5 to 14 for a given year is compared with the number 5 to 14 of the previous year to arrive at an index of migration for each county.

areas 1, 2, 5, and 9. Area 1 in the southeast contains a number of cities: Rochester, Red Wing, Winona, Austin, and Dakota and Washington Counties are suburban to the Twin Cities. Area 2 likewise has several cities of considerable size, while area 5 contains Anoka and Chisago Counties which are also influenced by being near the Twin Cities. Area 9 consists of Ramsey and Hennepin Counties and provides only slightly less than half of the total increase in the state during the period. It is clear that the cities are contributing the major portion of the increase in the state's population.

This fact is further borne out by the census of people living on farms which is reported annually by the state Department of Agriculture. From 1951 (when this census was taken for the first time) to 1958 the farm population declined from 645,819 to 579,765. The decline in farm population was greatest in the northern part of the state. This area, which is generally less suited to agriculture and therefore less productive, also has more opportunities for nonfarm employment. It is a forested area, where the acreage of cleared land per farm is small, often less than a fifth of the total. When nonfarm employment is available, the tendency is for farm operators to rent out their land and take full-time jobs in industry, and sometimes even to leave the area entirely and become town-dwellers. The farm population therefore increases in this area when nonfarm employment is not available. This results not so much from a back-to-the-farm movement as from the damming up on farms of people who would otherwise leave. In brief, the northern forested area acts as a sponge, absorbing population in bad times, and releasing it in good times.

Changes in age composition. Since 1920, the population has been increasing at the top and at the bottom: more people survive to older ages and more children are born. However, in the years before 1900 the proportion of children under 5 was very high — much higher than it is today. This reflects not only the large-family pattern of pioneer days, but also the youthfulness of the population in general. The immigrants were for the most part young or middle-aged. They were in the family-rearing years. Only 2.5 per cent were 65 or older in 1880, compared with 9 per cent in 1950. Those under 5 made up 15 per cent in 1880 and 11.1 per cent in 1950. The trend in proportions of people in various age groups is shown in Figure 6.

Changes in age and sex composition of the population can be more effectively shown by use of the pyramid of age and sex groups. It is useful

24

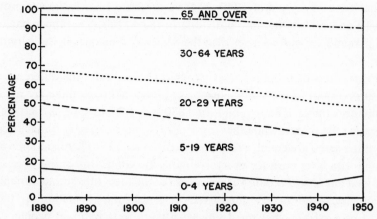

Figure 6. Percentage of Minnesota's Population in Various
Age Groups from 1880 to 1950

to compare the pyramids for 1950 and 1880 (Fig. 7). The graph for
1880 shows a comparatively young population and has a conical shape,
while that for 1950 shows an older population, and has more the shape
of a beehive. There are several points to note about the 1950 pyramid.
First of all, the bottom bar is very much longer than those above it. It
represents the very large rise in births during the period 1946–1950.
The bar next above it (5–9) is longer than the one next above, although
shorter than the bottom bar; these are the children born in the relatively

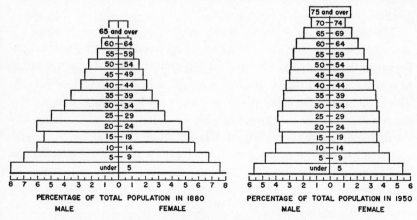

Figure 7. Age and Sex Distribution of Minnesota's
Population in 1880 and in 1950

25

higher birth-rate years of 1940–1945. The shortest bar is the age group 15–19 and reflects the low birth rate in the 1930's. The upper bars of the pyramid are much longer than the corresponding ones in the pyramid for 1880.

Proportions of the sexes. The pyramid also indicates the difference in the proportions of the sexes in each age group, although these are not so easily discernible. The pyramid for 1880 tends to bulge on the left, representing the males; while that for 1950 is almost perfectly symmetrical, since the sexes are equal, except for those under 15. (There are approximately 106 boys born for every 100 girls. However, this excess of males is wiped out in succeeding years because of the higher death rate of males at all ages.) Males constituted 61.2 per cent of the population in 1850. If we take a later date, say 1890 when there were 695,000 people, the male population still amounted to 53.7 per cent of the total. In other words there were 115 males to every 100 females.

Immigration tends to keep the ratio of males to females high. Among the foreign-born in 1890 there were 130 males per 100 females, and in 1950 the number was 118, although that of the native-born males was 100. The ratio of men to women tends to be high in the rural areas and low in the cities. For example, in 1950 there were 120 males per 100 females in the farm population, 103 in the rural nonfarm, and only 93 in the urban. In the age group 20–24 there were 145 males per 100 females on farms, 85 in the rural nonfarm (mostly villages under 2,500), and 84 in the urban. The corresponding figures for the age group 15–19 were 131, 97, and 83.

The reason for these disparities in the sex ratios by place of residence is migration. The girls are moving to villages and cities in greater numbers than the boys, particularly in the age groups 15–24. In the age group next older, 25–29, the ratio drops sharply to 112 men per 100 women. This drop may be the result of one or both of the following developments: the return of girls to the farm, probably after marriage to farm boys, and the increased migration of boys in this age group from farms.

The disproportion of the sexes in the 15–24 age group has a definite impact on marriage rates for men and women, a point which will be elaborated in the chapter on the family. It also raises questions about reasons for migration. Why do so many girls forsake the farms in Minnesota? The state ranks among the top six in the low proportion of women on farms.

26

Migration within Minnesota

The American people are noted for their tendency to move about and Minnesota conforms to the national pattern. Each year thousands of farm people move from farm to farm and other thousands leave the farm for villages, towns, and cities within the state and in other states. On the other hand, there are people who move to farms from villages, towns, and cities — a kind of reverse movement — but always of lesser size than the movement away from farms. Then there are the movements within and between villages, towns, and cities — and from one state to another.

The largest movement is away from the farms. We have already noticed the decline in the farm population and other indices which denote this movement. But the reduction in actual numbers of people on farms is only part of the story. To this must be added the large excess of births over deaths on farms, the so-called natural increase, in order to arrive at the total number of migrants. To illustrate: consider the farm population to be 900,000 at the beginning of a decade. Then assume the birth rate to be 25 per thousand and the death rate 10 per thousand, or a natural increase of 15 per thousand. Then this natural increase in any year is 900 times 15 or 13,500. This number could leave farms each year and the total population would remain the same — 900,000. Over a ten-year period the natural increase amounts to 135,000, which must be added to the number shown by the census to be the decline in the number on farms during the decade.

Migration into Minnesota from foreign lands and from other states has been declining over the years, as one might expect. The 1860 census showed that 80 per cent of the residents were born in other states or in foreign countries. By 1950 the foreign-born constituted 7 per cent, and those born in other states (568,145), combined with the foreign-born, made up only slightly more than one fourth (26 per cent) of the total. At the same time, Minnesotans left the home state for other states in large numbers. In 1950, 829,100 persons born in Minnesota — about 28 per cent of the population — were living in other states.

One of the interesting facts about the migrations of the American people is the tendency to follow lines of latitude. The movement has been overwhelmingly east to west. Thus the historical movement toward the west — to Minnesota — was from New England, New York, Ohio, Michigan, Wisconsin. Then as Minnesota lands were occupied, the roads still led westward to the Dakotas, Montana, and the far Northwest. Even in 1950 the pattern prevailed. The movement today is not a one-way road to the West. It is more properly an interchange of peoples between the Dakotas and Minnesota; or between Minnesota and its other border states of Iowa and Wisconsin. But the great magnets of population for the Upper Midwest are the Twin Cities and Duluth. To them are drawn the migrants from a vast interstate area.

Migration during 1940–1950. When migration occurs in large numbers it becomes a fact of great importance not only to the migrants, but to the communities they leave and those they go to. The migration of individuals or families has many motivations. There are both push and pull forces. For example, people leave the farm because they are not needed there to help with farm work: mechanization and other labor-savers have steadily reduced the need for manpower. Moreover, there is a consistently higher birth rate in farm population which makes too many hands for the available jobs. These are some of the forces that tend to push people off the farm.

The impact of migration on the communities of origin is evident in the adjustments that must be made in the institutional structure. The farm areas which have lost heavily have found it desirable and often necessary to abandon numerous schools and churches established when the population was larger. As will be noted in other parts of this book, the reorganization of school districts and the merging of town and country churches is in large measure due to the thinning out of the farm population resulting from migration.

Also, while the places of origin of the migrants are adjusting to declining numbers, the points of destination are put to the necessity of sheltering, feeding, and otherwise caring for increasing numbers. Wars always stimulate mass movements of the population as new industries arise to meet the war needs. But even in peacetime the rise of new industries and the expansion of established ones bring together large numbers of people from various places. The housing problems of urban-industrial complexes are familiar to all, as are the extraordinary needs for new schools and new churches, along with additional teachers, lawyers, doctors, and all the rest. Maladjustments and readjustments are the constant problems of communities most heavily affected by migration.

The small town's problem. "Is there anything we can do to keep our town alive?" asks the secretary of a Chamber of Commerce in a village

28

of around four hundred people. "Our community is steadily losing trade to Blanktown, 10 miles away. Our population declined by nearly 15 per cent between 1940 and 1950, while Blanktown gained by over 35 per cent and now has over 4,000 people." This complaint might be echoed by a third of the communities of Minnesota if they were all as concerned as this one over the fact that their population declined during the decade. As Table 3 shows, the small communities suffered most, and the smaller they were to begin with the greater their tendency to decline.

Table 3. Gain and Loss in Population of Incorporated Places between 1940 and 1950

Size of Place	No. of Places, 1940	No. Which Gained, 1940–1950	No. Which Lost, 1940–1950	Percentage Which Lost
Under 250..............	201	95	106	52.7
250–499	196	127	69	35.2
500–999	149	107	42	28.2
1,000–1,499	63	53	10	15.9
1,500–1,999	37	30	7	18.9
2,000–2,499	18	16	2	11.1
2,500–4,999	34	29	5	14.7
5,000–9,000	29	26	3	10.3
10,000–24,999	11	10	1	10.0
25,000 and over........	4	4	0	0.0
Total	743	497	245	33.0

Yet, in spite of the fact that so many small places lost population, there were actually more people living in them in 1950 than in 1940, a result quite largely due to the thirty-nine places newly incorporated during the decade and the increase in population of the small places which gained during the decade. The proportion of Minnesota's population living in incorporated places of under 5,000 is almost double that for the nation. But Minnesota is one of the "most incorporated" states of the Union because of its liberal legal provisions for incorporation. The nearly a fifth of the population of Minnesota in towns under 5,000 is about the same as that for the west north central region. Minnesota appears to be a favorable habitat for the small town, probably because of the great importance of the role such centers play in the economy of the region, serving as they do not only as dwelling places for millions of citizens, but also as service centers for the farm population around them. They are connecting links between the city and the farm.

Why do some towns grow while others decline? The reasons are undoubtedly various. In an effort to discover some of them, Edward W. Hassinger studied the trade centers in forty-three southern Minnesota counties, using data from the 1950 census. In general he found that distance from a larger center was a determiner of growth or decline during the decade 1940–1950. The small places (less than 2,000) which were within ten miles of larger centers (5,000 or more people) showed a greater tendency to lose or to fail to gain than those which were ten miles or more from such centers and not closer to other large centers. Those farther removed were apparently subjected to less competition from the larger places. Although rapid transportation and good roads have given farm families more choice among places to trade, apparently they still regard distance as an impediment.

One interesting difference from the general trend occurred in the case of places with under 400 population that were within ten miles of a place of 5,000 or more. Of these small places 68.2 per cent gained;[5] whereas of those of the same size group that were within ten miles of places from 2,000 to 4,999, only 23.5 per cent gained. It is quite probable that those in the neighborhood of the larger centers were functioning as suburbs — places of residence for people employed in the larger centers. Both size and distance from larger centers demonstratedly influenced the tendency of a town to gain or lose population during the decade.

The tendency to grow or decline in number is obviously not a matter of natural increase, but the result of mobility of people. While most people remain "immobile," there are always enough movers to result in a continuing redistribution of the population of the state. We have seen the steady shift of the population from farm to city over the past century, a clear result of the movement of people from place to place.

Is Farm-to-City Migration Selective?

The so-called rural exodus has been a cause for alarm for one reason or another for much of the past century, particularly in the 1900's. For one thing, it had long been regarded as axiomatic that the farm population was the repository of most of the virtues, while the city held most

[5] See Edward W. Hassinger, "Factors Associated with Population Changes in Agricultural Trade Centers of Southern Minnesota, 1940–50" (unpublished dissertation, University of Minnesota, 1958); and Edward W. Hassinger, "The Relationship of Trade-Center Population Changes to Distance from Larger Centers in an Agricultural Area," *Rural Sociology*, Volume 22, No. 2 (June, 1957), pp. 131–136.

of the vices and the social problems. For another, the farm population was regarded as the seedbed of the nation, from which came the recruits to keep the cities alive. For these and perhaps other reasons, it was considered vital to the national welfare that a good — though unspecified — portion of the total population should remain on the farm.

Since 1930 at least, these opinions have been greatly modified. The industrial prosperity of the 1920's, coupled with lack of it on the farm, resulted in heavy migration from the farms; but the depression of the 1930's impeded the normal movement of farm people from the farm to nonfarm jobs. There was talk then of people dammed up on farms, and the implication was that this was bad, and that what was good was for them to move out. Thus by mid-century, the talk was predominantly in favor of more and more people's leaving the farm and this movement was considered desirable. Not only was the "normal" movement out of farming to be applauded, but government programs, some believed, should encourage and accelerate the movement.

The alarm over farm-to-town migration has abated and the migration has come to be approved and encouraged, but there are still many who are not pleased with the consequences of the movement. "It is our well educated young people who leave us," they say. Or "This town suffers from a dearth of leaders because as fast as they are developed here, they move to the city." The old idea voiced so often a generation ago that the cream was being skimmed from the farm population implied a genetic deterioration, but this implication has not been proved. The inherent quality of the farm population is not considered to be any poorer as a result of migration than the quality of the city people.

Nevertheless it can be demonstrated that migrants differ in certain ways from the nonmigrating population. The characteristics on which we know the migration is selective are sex and age. How do we know? There are two main sources of evidence immediately available, both from the United States Bureau of the Census: one is the general census of population, the other the four special volumes on internal migration based upon the question asked in 1940 about place of residence in 1935. The first source can be used to compare the farm population by age and sex composition with the other groups in the population, the urban and rural nonfarm groups. When such comparisons are made, the selectivity as to age and sex becomes apparent.

Age. The farm population has a higher percentage of people under 15

31

and a smaller proportion of people from 15 to 60 than the other two groups. The difference can only be the consequence of migration. The large proportion of people in the middle ages in the urban population is the result of migration into the cities. The pyramid of total population assumes a conical shape, whereas the pyramid of the city population is more like a beehive. The inference is clear, therefore, that the city is receiving migrants from the town and country who are predominantly young.

The differences in age composition of the three segments of Minnesota's population are readily seen when the ratios of three age groups in the respective segments are computed (Table 4).

Table 4. Number of Urban, Rural Nonfarm, and Rural Farm Persons per 1,000 Population in Three Age Groups in 1940 and 1950

Age	State		Urban		Rural Nonfarm		Rural Farm	
	1940	1950	1940	1950	1940	1950	1940	1950
Under 20	339	348	300	313	343	360	397	414
20–64	585	562	624	595	559	525	539	520
65 and over....	76	90	76	92	98	115	64	66

Source: *United States Census of Population*, 1940 and 1950.

In what may be considered the working ages (20–64), the city has a marked advantage over the country. It is better supplied than the rural nonfarm, while the latter shows superiority over the farm group. Meanwhile, the farm has larger numbers of children to care for, although its proportion of aged is lower than either the urban or rural nonfarm; in this age group (65 and over) the villages show highest proportions because of the well-known tendency of retired farmers to live in them.

It is well to note the change from 1940 to 1950. The number and proportion of "dependent" groups — the younger and the older — have increased in all categories, but the differential between rural and urban remains.

The age-selective effect of migration from farms is further shown by data from the special report, published by the United States Bureau of the Census, *Internal Migration*. In Minnesota there were 48,328 males and 36,922 females in the farm population in 1940 who had moved since 1935. Some of them were urban in 1935, others had lived in rural nonfarm areas, some came from other farms, and still others came from other states and foreign countries. We are also able to determine from these data the number and characteristics (age, sex, education, and occupation) of the persons who lived on farms in 1935, but were in a new location in 1940.

The ages of rural farm migrants are compared with the ages of non-migrants in Table 5. The difference in age composition demonstrates the age selectivity of farm-to-city migration. The inferences to be drawn from Table 5 are these:

Table 5. Ages in 1940 of Rural Farm Migrants and Nonmigrants, by Sex

Age	Total		Male		Female	
	Migrants	Non-migrants	Migrants	Non-migrants	Migrants	Non-migrants
5–13	17.2%	21.1%	17.4%	20.6%	16.9%	23.2%
14–17	7.6	9.0	7.4	8.8	7.8	9.2
18–19	6.1	5.0	4.4	4.7	7.8	5.2
20–24	17.3	13.3	13.9	12.5	20.8	14.3
25–29	12.2	10.8	12.3	10.5	12.1	11.3
30–34	8.4	8.9	9.4	9.2	7.5	8.3
35–44	11.9	13.4	13.3	13.8	10.6	12.9
45–54	8.9	9.7	10.1	10.3	7.7	8.9
55–64	5.6	5.3	6.3	6.1	4.9	4.3
65 and over.....	4.7	3.0	5.4	3.5	4.0	2.4
Total	100.0	100.0	100.0	100.0	100.0	100.0

Source: United States Census of Population, *Internal Migration 1935–40; Social Characteristics of Migrants*, pp. 150–151; 247.

1. Migrants from Minnesota farms during the period, as compared with nonmigrants, were predominantly in the age groups from 18 to 30 and 55 and over; that is, in the younger working ages and in the retirement period.

2. The patterns for women and men migrants differ slightly. Women tend to leave earlier, beginning with ages 18–19, whereas the men show larger proportions over nonmigrants first in the age group 20–24. Moreover, the differences between proportions of migrants and nonmigrants at certain ages are greater for women. For example, in the age group 20–24, 20.8 per cent of the migrants are female, compared with 14.3 per cent of the nonmigrants. For the males in the same age group the figures are 13.9 per cent and 12.5.

Sex. There are significant differences in the proportions of males and females who leave the farm. This is shown by the differing proportions of

33

the sexes in the urban and rural sections as reported by the federal census. The simplest way to make this comparison is by means of the sex ratio, the number of males per 100 females. In Minnesota the ratios for the three population groups 15 years old and over in 1950 were urban, 90; rural nonfarm, 102; rural farm, 127. For the total population in this age group, the ratio was 105 men per 100 women. The differences are due to migration, in which the farm population loses women disproportionately and the cities get them. The ratio in the villages is about the same as that for the total population.

Turning briefly again to the data from the special report on internal migration, we find that for each 100 females 14 years of age and over who left Minnesota farms between 1935 and 1940 for the urban centers, there were only 72 males. Only four states had a higher proportion of women migrants: Mississippi, Nebraska, Wisconsin, and North Dakota. Of those who left farms for rural villages there were 92 males per 100 females; and again there were only four states with lower sex ratios: Rhode Island, Mississippi, Iowa, and North Dakota.

It is quite clear that cityward migration is selective on the basis of age and sex.

Education. As a rule, persons with high school education or more are more mobile than those with less schooling. Migrants from rural farm areas compared with nonmigrants showed the following differences: of the male migrants 25–34 years of age, 28.7 per cent had high school or more education, compared with 23.7 per cent of nonmigrants of the same age group. For females, the corresponding figures were 50.7 and 41.4 per cent.

Moreover, migrants differ in education according to their destination, urban or rural (Table 6). Usually, the larger the place to which farm migrants go, the higher their level of formal schooling. The migrants who went to the Twin Cities, for example, had the largest percentage with high school education or more; those listed as urban (which would include the Twin Cities) ranked next; those who went to rural nonfarm next; and those who went to other farm areas were lowest. This holds true for both males and females, although the disparity in the percentages for rural farm and the urban destinations is greater in the case of the males. Males who left farms for other farms during the period rated especially low on education with only 19.8 per cent educated beyond the eighth grade. The corresponding figure for female farm-to-farm migrants was

Table 6. Comparison of All Rural Farm Migrants Age 25–34 and Migrants with High School Education or More According to Destination, by Sex*

| | All Migrants | | Migrants with High School or More | | | |
| | | | Male | | Female | |
Destination	Male	Female	No.	%	No.	%
Twin Cities	1,330	1,378	698	52.5	903	65.5
All urban.......	1,827	1,787	787	43.1	1,067	59.7
Rural nonfarm ..	1,191	1,154	412	34.6	623	54.0
Rural farm......	3,800	3,049	742	19.8	1,241	40.7

Source: United States Census of Population, *Internal Migration 1935–40; Social Characteristics of Migrants*, pp. 150–151; 247.
*Migrants to Twin Cities include those from outside the state; all others are from within Minnesota.

Table 7. Migrants into the Twin Cities with High School Education or More from 1935 to 1940 by Origin and Sex*

| | High School Education or More | | | | | |
| | Twin Cities | | St. Paul | | Minneapolis | |
Origin	Male	Female	Male	Female	Male	Female
Other urban......	85.4%	87.1%	83.9%	85.1%	86.2%	88.1%
Rural nonfarm ...	76.4	83.4	74.2	81.4	77.4	84.3
Rural farm.......	52.5	57.4	46.9	60.1	55.1	66.4

Source: United States Census of Population, *Internal Migration 1935–40; Social Characteristics of Migrants*, pp.150–151; 247.
*All migrants, including out-of-state.

40.7 per cent. On the other hand, over half the males and about two thirds of the females who left farms for the Twin Cities were educated beyond the eighth grade. The marked difference between the education levels of males and females is also apparent.[6]

It is interesting to compare the rural farm migrants who came to the Twin Cities during this period with those originating in other urban or in rural areas (Table 7). For some unknown reason migrants into Minneapolis were relatively better educated than those who went to St. Paul; but the differences were not great, although consistent for all sources of migrants.

[6] For further information see Lowry Nelson, *Education of the Farm Population in Minnesota*, Minnesota Agricultural Experiment Station Bulletin No. 377; and Milo Peterson and Douglas Marshall, *Are Minnesota's Farm Youth in School?*, University of Minnesota Bureau of Educational Research and Agricultural Experiment Station, 1947 (mimeographed).

Distance of migration in relation to education can be measured roughly from the census data by comparing migrants within the state with those who went to contiguous and noncontiguous states: those who went to noncontiguous states ranked highest, with the intrastate migrants next (Table 8).

Table 8. Migrants from Minnesota Farms with High School Education or More According to Destination, by Sex

| | High School Education or More | |
Destination	Male	Female
Within Minnesota	43.1%	59.7%
Contiguous states..............	35.7	57.5
Noncontiguous states..........	43.4	61.7

Source: United States Census of Population, *Internal Migration, 1935–1940*.

There remains one other item which deserves attention in this brief treatment, and that is the education of those who moved from urban and rural nonfarm areas *into* the farm population. It is clear that migrants *from* the farms are generally better educated than those who remain. But it must be remembered that there is a back-flow of migrants from cities, towns, and villages to farms which partially offsets the farm-to-city movement. For example, 3,018 males and 2,941 females 25–34 years of age were living in towns and cities of Minnesota in 1940 who were on farms in 1935. But 1,716 males and 2,247 females were on farms in 1940 who were in towns and cities in 1935. There was a net loss in farm population in this exchange, but it is important to know how the education of those who entered the farm population compares with those who left the farms. On the whole the difference is not very great, but migrants to the farms seem slightly better educated than those who left (Table 9). Although the towns and cities get the better-educated persons from the farm population, they return somewhat better than they get. However, they return only slightly more than half as many as they received in this age group.

To sum up, migration from Minnesota's farm population is selective in age, sex, and education. Women are inclined to migrate earlier than men — over half of those who go to towns and cities are 14 to 24, while only a third of the men are in this age group.

There is little difference between the ages of male and female migrants who moved from one farm to another during the period under consideration. The sex ratio of the farm population in 1950 by age groups also reveals this age-sex selectivity. The ratio of the group 20–24 was 146. Minnesota farm population suffers an extraordinary loss of women through migration. It is outranked in this respect by only four other states.

The farm population tends to lose more of those with high school education or more. The metropolitan areas and the noncontiguous states get

Table 9. Percentages of Migrants with High School Education or More from and to Minnesota's Farm Population between 1935 and 1940, Urban and Rural Nonfarm, by Sex

| | High School Education or More | | | |
| | Urban | | Rural Nonfarm | |
Sex	To	From	To	From
Male	43.1%	46.1%	34.6%	40.0%
Female	59.7	63.2	54.0	59.6

Source: United States Census of Population, *Internal Migration, 1935–1940; Social Characteristics of Migrants*, pp. 150–151; 247.

those with most schooling, while migrants to smaller centers rank somewhat lower. Migrants from farm to farm, particularly the males, have markedly less education than those who go to towns and cities.

The country gets back from towns and cities migrants with slightly higher average education, but only a little more than half as many as left the farms.

The first resource to be used by the people of Minnesota was the land for the production of food and feed: the beginning of the state — as has been true of all human societies — was agricultural and rural. But the rise of nonagricultural occupations and industries was not long in coming. The division of labor was destined to become more elaborate and complex. And the growth of cities was destined to exceed that of the farm population. Indeed, the latter has steadily declined over the years, as the arts of plant and animal production have improved. This improvement in technology has resulted in extensive shifts in population, notably away from the farm.

The patterns of migration in Minnesota are extraordinary from the standpoint of sex selectivity. There are few states where women leave the farms in such numbers. Moreover, because of the relatively low rank of Minnesota's farm population in education beyond the eighth grade, the exodus of such large proportions of those with more education tends to increase the educational disparity between city and country — a disparity which can only be narrowed by heroic efforts to improve the attendance of farm boys and girls at high school, if not college. It is obvious that if all farm boys and girls were high school graduates, the difference in educational level of migrants and nonmigrants would disappear. Actually, it has disappeared in California and Utah, where attendance at school is required to age 18 or completion of high school. The school-leaving age in Minnesota is 16.

Some farm people in Minnesota were quick to relate their children's going to high school with their tendency to migrate. This dampened their enthusiasm for education beyond the elementary school. This question is discussed further in Chapter VI, where it is noted that the attitude toward high school education is somewhat related to the ethnic background of the parents. This in turn suggests the importance of considering the diverse cultural and ethnic streams which have formed the citizenry of the state. The chapter to follow is dedicated to that purpose.

III Of Kindreds, Tongues, and Peoples

THE people of Minnesota are the descendants of immigrants from nearly all the countries of the world. Because the census publishes only the important nationalities and lumps the remainder under "all others," it is impossible to know just how many different strains compose the state's population. Nevertheless, we know that the vast majority came originally from Europe.

National Origins

Although twenty-seven countries were listed in 1930 as contributing to the white population the great majority came from three countries: Germany, Sweden, and Norway. In short, if we include Finland and Denmark with these three nations, the total amounts to 70 per cent of the "foreign white stock" in 1930. At that time Scandinavian stock made up about 48 per cent of the total foreign white stock, and German 23 per cent. In 1910 the comparable percentages were 42.5 and 26.7. World War I no doubt accounted for the decline in German immigration.

Accurate count of people of any given descent is impossible. The census of 1930 was the last to provide us with two categories, *foreign-born* and *native-born of foreign-born parents*. Included are those with either one or both parents foreign-born. Later census enumerations have given us only the number of *foreign-born* by countries of origin. Since 1900 there has inevitably been an increasing proportion of the population who were native-born of native parentage, but these cannot be counted in the total stock of various national origins. Obviously the groups which were first to settle in the state — Germans, Swedes, Norwegians especially — would tend to have more descendants in the third generation or later category.

Censuses since 1930 have listed only the foreign-born by country of origin. But these figures still show the predominance of Germany, Norway, and Sweden, which have outranked all other nations consistently since 1880, with Germany in top position from 1860 to 1900. From 1910 to 1950, Sweden contributed the largest number of foreign-born, with Norway in second place each year except 1910 when Germany was second. Finland has ranked fourth in each census since 1920, except for 1950 when it was edged into fifth position by immigration from Canada.

Of course, the total numbers of foreign-born have been declining since the turn of the century. The reasons are to be found in the decline of economic opportunity in America for the immigrant — particularly in the disappearance of a chance to settle on the public domain — and in the passage in the 1920's of acts restricting immigration.

It is interesting to recall that Minnesota has long been regarded by dwellers in other states as the home of the Swedes. Yet it is quite clear from the available census data that Swedish stock is considerably outnumbered by German. They exceeded the foreign-born both from Sweden and from Norway each census year from 1860 to 1900. Moreover, in certain years Norwegian immigrants have outnumbered the Swedes. Naturally, if the Scandinavian countries are combined, the total immigration greatly exceeds that from Germany.

The question often arises as to what proportion of the population of Minnesota is of Scandinavian descent — including Norway, Sweden, Finland, Denmark, and Iceland. There is no way of knowing, of course, because no count could possibly be made of those of mixed descent, or of those who are born here of parents also born here. On the basis of the enumerations discussed above of foreign white stock, it would not be safe to place the Scandinavian stock at more than fifty per cent, and this would include those of mixed Scandinavian and partly non-Scandinavian parentage. The fact that so many people of this stock have been in the state from very early days of settlement means that there are now many more of them in the third generation and later than is true of the more recent immigrant groups. Moreover, it is possible that Minnesota has acted as a kind of magnet for native-born people of Scandinavian descent to move in from other states. This is admittedly a speculative estimate, but it is

40

reasonable to place a top limit of fifty per cent, and the true proportion of Scandinavians might be somewhat less (see Appendix).

Racial Groups Other Than White

The most numerous nonwhite people in Minnesota are Indians and Negroes. Their numbers have been roughly equal since 1870, when the census reported 759 Negroes and 690 Indians. By 1930 the Negroes numbered 9,445 and the Indians 11,072.[1] A marked increase in Negroes took place in the 1940's — from 9,928 to 14,022. The Indian population during this period remained about the same, at 12,533 in 1950, a gain of only 5 persons. It is well known that the Negro pattern of migration is from south to north. Little is known of the migratory behavior of the Indian. Since they are indigenous to Minnesota, migration from this area might well take place. Because the long-term trend of the Indian population shows very slow growth, and because it is not likely to be increased by migration into the state, the Negroes are likely to far outnumber them in the years ahead.

Japanese and Chinese have been noted in Minnesota for possibly a century. In 1880 the census reported 24 Chinese and 1 Japanese. Even ten years later, in 1890, there were only 2 Japanese — one wonders if he had brought his wife over. But in 1900 there were 51, and the numbers changed little until 1950 when the total reached 1,049, clearly a result of the expulsion of the Japanese from the Pacific Coast during the war. It is safe to say that most — if not all — were native-born and therefore American citizens. The Chinese showed a more steady and consistent growth to a total of 720 in 1950. Both groups are largely urban. What the census calls all other races — Filipinos, Hindustani, Koreans, and so on — made up a very small part of the Minnesota population (462 in 1950). This number has risen from decade to decade at an increasing rate, and it is to be expected that the increase will continue. The Filipinos are probably the most important numerically after the Japanese and Chinese. Although they are not enumerated separately by the census, a report by the Governor's Interracial Commission estimated that there

[1] The census count is regarded as inaccurate by the Governor's Interracial Commission. In their report to the governor appears this statement: "There is no exact count of Indian persons residing in Minnesota today . . . The State Health Department estimates Minnesota's Indian population, based on birth and death records, to be 13,688 persons. The Hoover Commission report published in 1949, in its study of the Indian problem at the federal level, estimated Minnesota's Indian population to be 18,000 persons." *The Indian in Minnesota* (revised) p. 33, 1952.

were 250 Filipino citizens of Minnesota in 1940, and probably between 300 to 500 people with some Filipino "heritage" living in the state.[2] The same report estimates that 90 per cent of the men are married to white women. Like the Chinese and Japanese they live mainly in the Twin Cities and Duluth.

Some Ethnic Differences Persist

Although assimilation of the various nationality groups is far advanced, evidences of the persistence of Old World values and customs are not difficult to find. One of the most obvious of these is the persistence of European languages. The 1940 federal census asked the people to report on the language commonly spoken at home in their earliest childhood: this was the mother tongue. These were reported by three categories of people: foreign-born, native-born of foreign or mixed parentage, and native-born of native parents. The last category contains those who were of the third generation or more in this country. For all those of whatever national origin or background in Minnesota who reported a mother tongue other than English to the census-taker, nearly 26 per cent were third generation or later. There were seventeen states with higher percentages, but most of them with rather low numbers of people in the population who reported a mother tongue other than English. There were wide differences among nationality groups, as Table 10 shows. All of the groups also differ according to whether they were dominantly urban or rural.

Use of Old World tongues. In 1940 there were 875,740 persons, or about 30 per cent of the total population of the state, who reported a mother tongue other than English. About 27 per cent of these were foreign-born, 55 per cent were native-born of foreign or mixed parentage, and about 18 per cent were native-born of native parents. A measure of the varying persistence in some groups of their tongue over others may be indicated by comparing the percentages which still report the use of an Old World tongue, even though native-born of native-born parents. This is not an infallible measure, however, because the more recent immigrants, such as the Italians, the Yiddish-speaking peoples, the Slovenians, and the Russians, would inevitably have more of their numbers in the first two groups; foreign-born and native of foreign or mixed parentage. Nevertheless, when Swedes, Norwegians, Danes, Dutch, and Ger-

[2] *The Oriental in Minnesota,* a report by the Governor's Interracial Commission, 1949.

mans — groups which have been long in the state and who came at about the same time — are compared, it is useful to note differences in the persistence of Old World tongues in the third generation and later. The differences among the Scandinavian groups are particularly interesting. The Norwegians show a persistence rate about three times that of the Swedes and Danes. Important here may be the fact that a larger percentage of the Swedes settled in the cities, while the immigrants from Norway have gone to the land. Another explanation may lie in the stronger cultural bonds existing in the Norwegian group. Perhaps their long subordination to both Sweden and Denmark until their emancipation in 1905 developed in them a stronger in-group feeling, which has helped to preserve their cultural identity in the New World. Then too, they came to Minnesota when land was available for settlement. They became farm people, settling near each other for the most part, where communication with each other was easy, and where they could maintain their own churches without the inconvenience of accommodating themselves to outsiders.

Yet the Norwegians show much less persistence than the Germans, French, and Czechs. These, too, are old settlers, very few are foreign-born (Table 10); yet large percentages of the native-born of native parents report the use of foreign languages. They also have tended to group themselves in tightly knit islands, both on the land and in the towns and cities. This grouping has often been encouraged by the existence in their midst of their historical ethnic churches, whether Protestant or Catholic.

It will be seen from Table 11 that of the total population reporting Old World mother tongues, around 40 per cent were in the urban and rural farm categories and the balance in the rural nonfarm. Since we are interested especially in the native-born of native parents, it is instructive to discover the proportions of such persons who were urban and rural. My hypothesis is that the language tends to persist more strongly in the rural areas than in the urban, and most strongly in the farm territory. There is no point in including the Yiddish, Russian, and Italian language groups here, since their numbers are small and very few are farmers. Table 11 shows that there is a consistent upward gradient in the percentages from urban to rural nonfarm to rural farm. The Danes and the Dutch show slightly higher proportions in rural nonfarm than in the rural farm, but in no case is the urban rate higher than either. Similar calculations were made for the United States, with the same general trend in evidence. One must conclude from these data that the social metabolism of the city as-

Table 10. Number of Minnesotans by Language Groups Who Reported Mother
Tongues Other Than English and Percentage Distribution by
Nativity and Residence

Language	Total	Urban	Rural Nonfarm	Rural Farm	Foreign-Born	NB, F or M*	NB, NB†
Norwegian	193,340	34.0%	19.4%	46.6%	24.6%	58.2%	17.1%
Swedish	164,560	51.3	14.8	33.9	39.9	54.3	5.8
Danish	22,620	42.8	17.5	39.7	45.7	48.9	5.3
Dutch	11,980	16.4	18.2	65.4	34.7	51.4	13.8
French	23,400	52.5	17.3	30.2	18.9	51.6	29.6
German	293,560	33.5	20.0	46.5	16.9	54.8	28.3
Polish	40,880	55.7	10.1	34.2	24.3	57.9	17.8
Czech	28,700	27.7	19.9	52.4	19.6	52.1	28.3
Slovenian	13,920	65.8	24.7	9.5	33.3	64.7	2.0
Russian	7,380	84.8	5.7	9.5	56.6	39.6	3.8
Finnish	50,240	32.8	15.1	52.1	34.4	55.4	10.2
Yiddish	12,300	98.0	1.8	0.2	58.2	40.2	1.6
Italian	12,860	80.4	17.3	2.3	42.9	53.7	3.4
Total	875,740	40.8	17.6	41.6	26.9	55.1	17.9

Source: 16th Census of the United States, *Population, Nativity, and Parentage of the White Population; Mother Tongues*, Table 3.
*Native-born of foreign or mixed (one native-born, the other foreign-born) parentage.
†Native-born of native-born parents.

Table 11. Percentage of Minnesota People in 1940 Who Were Native-Born of
Native Parents and Used Another Tongue at Home, by Area of Residence

Language	Total	Residence		
		Urban	Rural Nonfarm	Rural Farm
Norwegian	17.1%	9.1%	16.3%	23.4%
Swedish	5.8	4.5	6.9	7.3
Danish	5.3	4.5	6.1	5.8
Dutch	13.8	6.1	16.5	15.1
French	29.6	22.6	35.6	38.3
German	28.3	17.1	27.2	36.8
Polish	17.8	9.5	19.8	30.8
Czech	28.3	11.3	29.7	36.8
Slovenian	2.0	0.6	3.5	7.6
Finnish	10.2	4.5	10.5	13.6
Total	17.9	9.6	18.9	25.6

Source: 16th Census of the United States, *Population, Nativity, and Parentage of the White Population: Mother Tongues*, Table 3.

44

similates Old World groups more rapidly than does that of the towns or the rural farm communities.

Marriage within the Ethnic Group

The ultimate test of assimilation is intermarriage. If marriage partners are chosen exclusively, or even predominantly, from the same ethnic group, the mother tongue and various cultural traditions are more likely to be preserved. On the other hand, if the marriage partners are from different ethnic groups, their respective languages are less likely to be transmitted to the children, and the parents themselves will tend to use them less. Because marriage is the crucial test of assimilation, I have assembled some data over the years — mainly as by-products of other research — which indicate the trend in marriage choices by nationality groups. The data are presented in Table 12.

The data from Wright County were gathered in 1942 during a survey which had as its central object the delineation of rural neighborhoods. Questionnaires were obtained through the rural ungraded schools, which

Table 12. In-Group Marriage in Certain Ethnic Groups in Three Samples of Minnesota Farmers

Ethnic Group	Wright County (1942)		Northeastern Counties (1956)		Clay County (1954)	
	No.	Spouse Same Nationality	No.	Spouse Same Nationality	No.	Spouse Same Nationality
German	385	80.0%	92	44.6%	75	38.7%
Norwegian	22	18.2	81	45.7	122	46.7
Swedish	195	61.8	70	30.0	21	19.0
Finnish	83	86.7	71	77.5	...	...
French	54	48.1	...	...	...	...
Irish	43	23.2	17	29.4	11	27.3
Polish	34	73.5	...	...	...	...
English	27	59.2	16	18.8	...	...
Dutch	24	58.3	...	...	...	...
Bohemian	18	50.0	...	...	...	...
Others*	...	...	61	29.5	18	22.2
Totals and averages.	885	68.2	408	32.3	247	41.7

Sources: Lowry Nelson, "Intermarriage Among Nationality Groups in a Rural Area of Minnesota," *American Journal of Sociology*, Vol. XLVIII, No. 5 (March, 1943), 589; unpublished data for northeastern counties and Clay County, in the Rural Sociology office, University of Minnesota.
*Includes Czech, French, Bohemian, Dutch, Austrian, Belgian, Slavonian, Yugoslavian, Polish, Scotch, Welsh, Swiss, Lithuanian, Russian, and English.

in addition to other information secured the nationality of the father and of the mother of the pupils. The presumption is that most if not all of the husbands were farmers, although the schedule did not ask for occupation.

The sample reported in the second column of Table 12 was surveyed in 1956 and consisted of 533 farm operators scattered throughout the thirteen northeastern counties of the state. Again, this study had a major objective of discovering the social and economic characteristics of the farmers in the Cutover, and information as to the ethnic identity of husband and wife was incidental. In the table, only the men who were not of mixed ethnic descent were included. In other words, of 533 men in the survey there were 125 who were of mixed ethnic origin.

The Clay County group consisted of 351 farm operators, of whom 104 were of mixed descent and are not included in the table. The purpose of this survey was to determine the characteristics of participators in agricultural extension work. In Wright County eighteen or more husbands were reported from each ten nationality groups. Lesser numbers were reported from the Belgian, Danish, Swiss, and Austrian nationalities; these are not included in Table 12, which shows the percentages of the husbands that had married within their own groups. It should be added that all of those reporting a mixed or American parentage were excluded from the tabulations, but these were few. There is wide variation, of course, among the groups in their tendency toward intermarriage; those who seem least inclined to intermarry are the Germans, Finns, and Poles. No information was gathered about the birthplaces of these parents of rural schoolchildren, but it seems fairly safe to assume that they are of the second, third, or later generation in the United States. These parents are most likely classifiable as rural farm population, since their children are attending ungraded rural schools. As we have seen from the data on the mother tongue, languages are more likely to persist among rural farm than among urban or rural nonfarm groups. In the case of Wright County, the numerical importance of certain groups in the population makes possible choosing a spouse of the same nationality. Where numbers of a certain group are small, the likelihood is greater that a spouse may be chosen from outside that group.

Among the farm operators in northeastern Minnesota in 1956, twenty-one different nationalities were represented. Here again, as in Wright County, the Finns showed the strongest tendency toward choosing mates in their own group. The Germans and Norwegians followed.

In Clay County in northwestern Minnesota a rather marked preference for in-group marriage was evidenced among people of German and Norwegian descent, with lesser percentages among Swedes, Irish, and others. Here again the numerical predominance of the German and Norwegian groups probably had much to do with the high percentages. The percentage of the total 351 couples who were ethnically alike was only 27.8, but for those who were not of mixed parentage the percentage was 41.7. In this sample, we have the ages of the women who were interviewed and provided the information on nationality of their husbands, but these data are not included here. While the differences were not large, generally those 21 to 34 years of age reported endogamous marriages at the rate of 20.7 per cent; from 35 to 44, 20.8 per cent; 50 to 65, 41 per cent. Of those 65 years of age and over, only 23.5 per cent reported endogamous marriages. In this group, however, the number was small, only 17. Even so, their percentage of in-group marriage was higher than that of the younger people and this may be regarded as least as an indication of the growing tendency among younger people toward intermarriage.

Religion and Assimilation

Organized religion in Minnesota is in many cases practically identical with ethnic groups and tends to reinforce cultural cohesion. Often in the past the languages of immigrants were kept alive through conducting services in the Old World tongues. The churches provided the immigrant with a haven of familiarity against the culture shock of the strange New World. Here he could sing the hymns in his own tongue, listen to sermons he could understand, and read the Scriptures in the language he had always known. The translation of hymns into English, and the Scriptures as well, meant the loss of the emotional overtones which he experienced when they were rendered in his own language. It has often required several generations to make the transfer from the old language to the new in the case of religious observance. It seemed logical, therefore, to assume that religion would have a pronounced effect on the choice of marriage partners; that the church whose members consisted predominantly of a particular group would encourage marriage within the church members. There is no adequate body of data to test this assumption, but a comparison of ethnic in-group marriages between Protestants and Roman Catholics may be made.

47

THE MINNESOTA COMMUNITY

In 1956, 1,675 seniors in twenty Minnesota high schools were asked to provide information to the department of rural sociology at the University of Minnesota on many questions about their future plans and hopes. Sixteen of the high schools were in the thirteen northeastern counties and four in the southwestern corner of the state.

Incidental to the general survey, the seniors were asked to tell the nationality background of their fathers and mothers, their religious affiliation, and whether they lived in town or country. There were 1,645 usable schedules returned. Based on these data, Table 13 was constructed

Table 13. Parents of 1,645 High School Seniors Who Married within the Same Ethnic Group, by Religion and Residence, 1956*

Residence	No.	Total	Catholic	Protestant
Town	1,069	20.4%	17.9%	21.2%
Area I	498	21.1	17.2	22.4
Area II	409	17.4	20.0	16.4
Area III	163	25.8	14.3	28.9
Open country	576	24.3	28.3	23.3
Area I	183	25.7	10.5	27.4
Area II	283	21.6	23.9	20.8
Area III	121	25.6	46.4	19.4
Total	1,645	21.8	20.9	21.9

Source: Survey of High School Seniors, 1956, Department of Rural Sociology, Institute of Agriculture, University of Minnesota.
*Areas I and II were east and west sections of the 13 northeastern counties; Area III consists of the southwestern counties known as the Corn Belt.

to show the proportion of the parents in each subgroup who were ethnically alike. There is practically no difference between the Catholic and Protestant groups with regard to intermarriage among ethnic categories. Only 21.8 per cent of the total were of the same background, with neither parent "mixed." There was a large difference between Catholics and Protestants in area III, open country; but this is likely due to the influence in that area of cultural islands of German Catholics who live on farms.

About half of the 1,645 couples were "mixed"—that is, one or the other of the spouses was. If the "mixed" are left out of consideration and only the "pure" used, 44.3 per cent of these couples were of the same nationality. The Finns ranked highest with 77.8 per cent; the Czechs had 66.7; the Germans 50.4; the Norwegians 42.9; the Poles 40.9; and the Swedes 40.4.

Propinquity and Assimilation

The rate of assimilation of ethnic groups obviously differs widely, and this inspires questions about why the differences exist. Some ethnic groups have formed themselves into cultural islands and have thereby created a certain amount of isolation. A study of the population of Minnesota shows definitely that persons of German descent are heavily concentrated in Stearns and adjacent counties and along the Minnesota River in southwestern Minnesota. The people of Norwegian descent predominate in much of the Red River Valley, and they are also dominant in some of the other southern counties, such as Fillmore, Goodhue, Houston, and Dodge. The Finnish people form high proportions of the population of the northeastern counties. Where such heavy concentrations of an ethnic group exist, it is much easier to keep alive their mother tongue, to marry within the group, and to preserve some Old World customs. As late as the 1940's it was possible to map the concentrations of twenty nationality groups on the basis of their constituting more than half of the population of their respective areas. The color map constructed by Douglas G. Marshall and published in the *Minneapolis Sunday Tribune* of August 28, 1949, shows an interesting mosaic of the hard cores of ethnic cultures. (The original of the map is in the rural sociology department of the University of Minnesota.) While urban centers and even towns and villages are not without their clustering of ethnic groups, there the groups live close to other groups and must learn to communicate with the other groups, which usually means learning English, and there the possibility is greater that their young people will intermarry.

Groups Differ in Desire to Assimilate

The behavior of immigrant groups may assume various patterns. They may resist accepting the values and ways of living of the enveloping culture. Examples of this are some of the pietistic religious groups – the Old Order Amish in Pennsylvania, Ohio, and Indiana, and the Hutterites in North Dakota, Montana, the Canadian prairie provinces, and, recently, western Minnesota. Such groups seek above everything else to keep from accepting the values of the outside world. Some other groups, including the Poles, Bohemians, and Finns in Minnesota, constitute minorities in certain sections and for various reasons wish to preserve their Old World customs. They are bilingual, often conduct meetings in

49

the Old World tongue, but shift readily to the English language if an outsider is present.

On the other hand, the larger culture may attempt to prevent the minority group from being assimilated by various devices such as excluding them from membership in groups and organizations and refusing to allow them to buy or hold property. Minnesota has a special problem with the American Indians. National policy from the beginning has forced this group into restricted areas, deprived them of certain rights and privileges, and at the same time tried to get them to accept the religion of the white Americans, to learn the English language, and to educate their children in the American kind of school. When they leave the reservation their opportunities for employment are frequently very scarce and they suffer from certain other discriminatory practices in the process of adapting to the world outside the reservation.

Immigrant Organizations and Assimilation

The early immigrants sought to preserve their way of life in the New World by creating various kinds of secular organizations. Some formed lodges or mutual aid groups; others emphasized musical and gymnastic associations. It is understandable for people from the same country and even from the same province within their country to endeavor to settle near each other and to form associations based upon their common place of origin. This is a phenomenon common to the United States and to other countries — including Latin America — which attracted European immigrants.

Although the evidence of persistence of these Old World traits is still manifest in Minnesota, it is reasonable to expect that over the generations, these traits will become less apparent. While our data on intermarriage are not conclusive as to trend because they are from different areas and from different time periods, they indicate a decline in the proportion of marriages within ethnic groups. Some groups more than others will retain for a long time to come a hard core of ethnic identity. Others will continue to lose their social visibility rapidly and become a part of the mass society.

The Social Significance of Ethnic Differences

That there are differences among the ethnic groups of Minnesota should be no cause for alarm. The numerous groups from all parts of the world which compose the population of the state have all brought with them contributions from their homelands. They have added much interest and color to the life of the state. These very facts of diversity of backgrounds and the necessity for all groups to get along with each other have been excellent discipline in tolerance and cooperation.

Yet all the lessons of living together amicably have not been fully learned. And not all members of the various groups are as far along the road of tolerance as some others are. Ethnic differences have been the basis of discrimination and even persecution at times. A conspicuous example of the latter was the unjust treatment of citizens of German descent during World War I. Also, in subtle ways, some groups are less firm than others in the support of major institutions, such as the public schools, and of government policies which affect adversely the people of the land from which they came. These differences will cease after a time to be critical matters; history up to now has shown much change for the better. It should be recognized by all citizens that there are groups which hold values that at times do not permit them to conform to majority regulations. There are those, for example, who do not believe in war as a means of settling international disputes. As a matter of conscience they refuse to perform military service or to buy war bonds. Happily, arrangements have been made to permit conscientious objectors to serve the country in others ways than in direct military service.

But in less conspicuous ways than feelings against pacificism, some groups have manifested intolerance of others. For example, citizens of Russian origin are presently suspected in some quarters of being Communists, as there are those who may be suspected of being Nazis or Fascists. Intergroup tensions based upon suspicion of sympathy with one or another of these ideologies have characterized the recent past. Such suspicions are obviously not limited to ethnic groups, but the fact that three countries are, or were, dominated by one or the other of these "isms" gives the problem a nationality identification.

Some immigrant stocks have shown a greater tendency than others to engage in agriculture, perhaps, because they came when land was readily available under the Homestead Act or other land acts which permitted acquisition of farms under favorable circumstances. People of German descent have attached themselves strongly to farming, and their time of immigration coincided with the period when original settlement was taking place. This was also true of the Norwegian and Swedish immigration.

51

But the earliest settlers also included old American stock from the settled portions of the United States — New York, Pennsylvania, Ohio, and the New England states. Irish immigrants were early on the scene also. But among these major ethnic stocks, the Germans and Norwegians have shown the greatest tenacity for farming. For example, in a study of the land ownership of a township in Minnesota from 1860 to 1948, Marian Deininger and Douglas G. Marshall found that the settlement was overwhelmingly Anglo-American in 1860, with only a small proportion of Germans. Specifically, the Old Americans owned nearly 70 per cent of the land of the township in 1860, the Irish 6.6 per cent, and the Germans 4 per cent. By 1948 the Germans owned 40 per cent, the Old Americans 35 per cent, and the Irish 3.2 per cent. Obviously, the Germans have a stronger commitment to agriculture than does either of the other groups.[3]

The Norwegians have shown a stronger tendency to remain in agriculture than have the Swedes. The Swedes have urbanized more readily and have intermarried with other groups more than the Norwegians have, from all we can tell from admittedly meager data available. I have already shown in this chapter that the Swedes have not retained their native language to the extent that the Norwegians have. It may be worthy of note in this connection also that the Norwegian Lutheran Church (now the Evangelical Lutheran Church) in the *Census of Religious Bodies: 1936*, ranked second among churches with 100,000 or more members in the proportion of its people who were rural. It reported 70 per cent rural membership while by contrast the Augustana Lutheran Synod, made up predominantly of people of Swedish origin, reported only 36 per cent rural, giving it rank of 25th in a list of 36 denominations.[4]

Other groups of lesser numerical importance than the Germans have also exhibited a tradition favorable to farming. Among these are the Poles, the Bohemians, and the Dutch. All have shown unusual success as farmers. This is not to say that other nationalities, including the various Scandinavian groups and the Anglo stocks, have not also shown marked aptitudes for farming. However, some groups have shown more interest in nonagricultural occupations than others and have encouraged their children to go into the professions, business, and trades to a greater extent.

[3] Marian Deininger and Douglas G. Marshall, "A Study of Land Ownership by Ethnic Groups from Frontier Times to the Present in a Marginal Farming Area in Minnesota," *Land Economics*, Vol. 31, No. 4 (November, 1955), pp. 351–360.

[4] Bureau of the Census, *The Census of Religious Bodies: 1936*, Washington, D.C.

Possibilities for Research

The trend toward assimilation of various ethnic groups could be observed by periodically repeating the survey of Wright County referred to earlier in this chapter. A similar recheck might be made of the Clay County people after a lapse of, say, ten years. Perhaps more important would be a follow-up study of ethnic groups in communities asked in the early 1950's about secondary education for their children. While most of these data have never been published, they remain in the files of the rural sociology department of the University of Minnesota and can be used as a benchmark against which to measure changes.

Unfortunately, it is impossible to continue the analysis of use of other languages because the census no longer asks for this information, although it is possible to use other sources of information, including the reports of various churches on the language used in services. Studies of the responses of the various ethnic groups to such institutions as the Agricultural Extension Service are also valuable contributions to an understanding of their place in our society now and in the future.

In conclusion it may be appropriate to observe that the process of assimilation is not always in one direction. Sometimes social crises like war or even a severe depression reverse the process. Human beings tend to seek a scapegoat. Historically, the Jews have most often been the unfortunate victims of this propensity, but the Christians, the Roman Catholics, and other groups have shared the persecution. Under crisis conditions minority groups which are well on the way to assimilation may suddenly once again become socially visible and be exposed anew to manifestations of intolerance. At such times it becomes the high task of statesmanship and leadership to anticipate and forestall, as far as possible, evil consequences.

Minnesota's society is but a century old. It is composed of people of diverse origins. There have been few episodes in her history to reverse the steady process of assimilation, which has gone forward peacefully and with tolerance, but there have been some. Much diversity should be allowed, so long as unity is preserved on issues that require the common effort for survival.

IV Families Old and New

THE family is the only major social institution that has a predetermined end; like human beings, families are born and die. No such preordained cycle characterizes governments, churches, or educational institutions. Their members come into them and pass out, according to their personal life cycles, but the life cycle of the institution is not visibly affected. Not so with the family; it is geared to the birth, maturation, decline, and demise of its members. Of course, the family as an institution is an ongoing concern, but the individual family runs its inevitable cycle from marriage through the various stages, dictated by birth and growth of children, to the empty nest and the death of the founding partners. Thus it is common to speak of one of the old families, and refer to individuals as members of one of the pioneer families of the state. The family as an institution is ongoing also in the cultural patterns which condition its form — monogamy, polygamy, and so on — and prescribe the norms of behavior for its members. In referring to "old" families we are speaking of a family line or lineage, not of a specific nuclear family. It is the latter with which we are concerned in this book, at the same time recognizing the continuities in kinship, of family groups which trace their lineage back to earlier times.

Through the institution of marriage and the miracle of reproduction, society is continually regenerated. Each year currently from twenty-five to thirty thousand marriages are contracted in Minnesota. The number in any year depends upon the size of the population and the influence of various factors — some known and some not known — that induce

54

people to marry. The marriage rate fluctuates around nine or ten per thousand population. If this rate held approximately in 1850 when there were 6,077 people, there would have been from 55 to 65 marriages. Then, as the population grew, the number rose accordingly. So we can picture the endless series of half circles endlessly overlapping in time, each half circle representing the families which began at a given year, the circle rising from a base line to its zenith and declining to the base line again. This mass of overlapping half-moon curves at any point in time is composed of families some of which are just beginning, some with all the children under six years of age; some with older children, but none over fourteen, some with all the children past the grade schools and in high school or college or both; some with all the children gone from the parental home — married or otherwise away, and some in the empty nest stage, with the parents in the final years of life.

This infinite overlap of beginnings and endings of families accounts for the complex age composition of a society at a given time. It also lies at the foundation of many of the numerous tensions in society among its diverse age groups and the conflicting interests in such fields as education, government, and welfare. Those who are preoccupied with the welfare of children view the world differently from those whose children are grown and gone — or those who never had any.

This commentary on the unique character of the family among social institutions is preliminary to the well-worn statement that the family is the basic unit of society. This eternal and infinite routine of entrances and exits of family groups provides not only the regeneration and rejuvenation of society, but makes indispensable numerous other institutions to condition, train, and control the human fledglings as they grow up. Thus, there must be schools, churches, governments, and all the other social institutions.

Because the family lies so close to the core of our system of values, the other social institutions in many ways serve as protectors of and aids to the family in fulfilling its functions. For example, while men may strive to accumulate wealth for its own sake or for such ends as prestige and power, the vast majority regard wealth as a means for reaching goals of security and well-being of the family. Thus, a major goal of agricultural policy is the preservation of the family farm because such a farm is considered best for the family. And not only is the family farm a major goal, but the ownership thereof is also sought. Ownership, according to the prevailing belief, provides the greatest measure of security for the family. Security and well-being require many things, not all of them material. Indeed, the main concerns of parents after the basic wants of the children are satisfied consist of rearing the children so that there might be some assurance that they will become well-adjusted and happy adults. The great concern of society is that the children born into the family grow up to become useful, law-abiding, and creative adults. To an increasing extent, parents are concerning themselves with the social and psychological aspects of their job. Parents living on farms are as much preoccupied with the noneconomic aspects of childrearing as those in the cities and towns.

Traditionally, the country has been regarded as the ideal habitat for family life. This is so thoroughly embedded in the American value system as to need no argument: most persons would accept it as true without asking for scientific proof. Farm life, the reasoning goes, provides greater opportunity for children to learn about nature; the country offers space for them to play and to have adventures in caves, streams, and woods. They can more readily learn the discipline of work by having chores to do even in their very early years. They can learn more about more things, and thus learn to be resourceful and self-reliant. These are the arguments.

However, the facts do not all support this proposition. A little thought should suggest that it is too idyllic to suppose that the farm family experiences no conflicts and is subjected to no stresses. It is true that the statistics indicate a lower divorce rate among farm people, but this is subject to some qualification because of a tendency of unknown magnitude for divorced persons, particularly women, to migrate to the town and city, and the tendency of the men to remarry. Thus, the facts on divorce gathered at any particular time cannot tell the whole story.

Composition of the Farm Family

But without entering into the argument of farm versus city as a place to rear children, it may be well to introduce the general discussion of the Minnesota family by summarizing the data on marital status as revealed by the census. We are concerned here only with the population which was 14 years old or over at the time of the 1950 census. Table 14 shows that a higher proportion of males than females in the urban population are married, in spite of a larger proportion of single men. The difference is explained by the extraordinary percentage of widowed and divorced females in the city, a fact which distorts the percentages in the other categories. In the farm population the percentage of married women greatly exceeds that of married men. This is related to the great excess of men on the farm, just as the excess of women in the city population makes for a high proportion of married men. That is, there are more

Table 14. Sex and Marital Status of Minnesota's Population 14 Years and Older by Residence, Compared with the Whole United States, 1950

Sex and Marital Status	United States	Minnesota	Urban	Rural Farm	Rural Nonfarm
Male					
Single	26.2%	29.6%	26.5%	37.7%	27.1%
Married	67.8	64.7	67.3	58.3	66.5
Widowed or divorced	6.0	5.7	6.2	4.0	6.4
Female					
Single	20.4	22.7	24.8	20.7	18.6
Married	65.5	64.9	60.9	72.5	68.7
Widowed or divorced	14.1	12.4	14.3	6.8	12.7

Source: *United States Census of Population: 1950.*

opportunities for women to marry on the farm and for men to marry in the city. The low percentage of widowed and divorced persons in the farm population and the correspondingly high proportions in the rural nonfarm and urban populations is due in large part to the tendency of such persons to move to town. The rural nonfarm population ranks between city and farm on all counts save one: there are more widowed and divorced men in the nonfarm population.

A point of some interest in connection with marital status is that there was an increase during the decade in the percentage of persons 14 and over who were married. In 1940 the married group made up 57.9 per cent of the total, while in 1950 the percentage was 64.8. This remarkable change may be accounted for as follows:

During the depression of the 1930's those of marriageable age tended to postpone matrimony. Then when employment opportunities and wages increased after 1940, many of these persons married. The outbreak of war also precipitated a rush to the altar as a possible hedge against the draft, plus the desire to wed before the war took the man away. There were also extraordinary numbers of people of marriageable age in the population, a result of the very large baby crops of the early 1920's (see

57

Fig. 8). Observers of the middle 1950's can see a reverse trend. As the children of the low-birth years of the 1930's come to marriageable age, there is a distinct drop in the marriage rate.

Size. Not only are more Minnesota people married, they are having more children and having them at younger ages. This is a recent development. Minnesota's birth rate fell from 24.7 per 1,000 population in 1915 to 16.8 in 1933 (see Fig. 8). Comparable rates for the United States are 25.0 and 16.6. After 1933 the rate rose steadily but gradually to 19 per 1,000 population in 1940. After that the rise became more marked. Even in 1945, the lowest year after the beginning of World War II, the birth rate was higher than at any time in the 1930's. Although somewhat lower than the peak year of 1947, the rate in 1950 was a hefty 25.2 and it has remained in that neighborhood in subsequent years. The trend of birth rates for the United States was the same as for Minnesota, but the rates were usually lower. The United States birth rate in 1940 was 17.9, somewhat less than the Minnesota rate of 19. Subsequent yearly rates for the United States have also averaged less than those for Minnesota. For example, the Minnesota rate in 1945 was 20.7, compared with 19.5 for the nation. By 1957 the rates were respectively 25.9 and 25. As has been pointed out earlier, the declining death rate which has accompanied the rising birth rate has resulted in a very large natural increase.

The important fact in discussing the Minnesota family, however, is the persistence of the high birth rate. This has been difficult to explain and was not anticipated by students of population. It was expected, naturally, that the birth rate would rise with the increased marriage rate — which resulted from causes mentioned above — but it was supposed that after the first and second births, or perhaps the third, the rate would decline and approximate the prewar rate. The fact that it has held high for over ten years means that there has been an increase in the fourth, fifth, and even sixth births. In short, the size of families has increased over that of the previous generation. There are more children under 5 per 1,000 women aged 15 to 44 years in the Minnesota population than at any time since 1910 (see Table 15).

Rural populations both farm and nonfarm contain relatively more children than does the urban. This has long been true; but the difference was less in 1950, for example, than it was in 1920 for both Minnesota and the nation. In 1920 the number of children in rural farm families

58

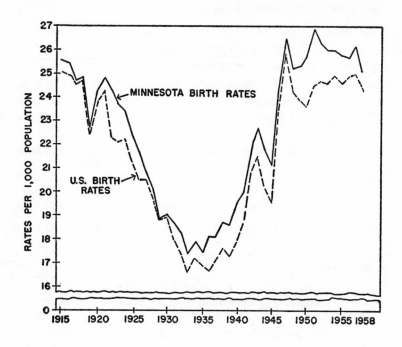

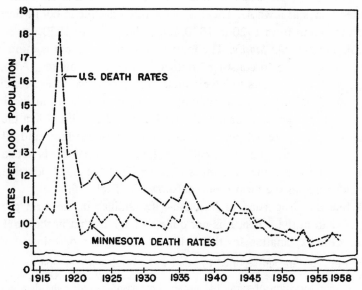

Figure 8. Crude Birth and Death Rates in Minnesota and
in the United States from 1915 to 1958 (1958
figures are provisional)

was 62 per cent greater than in urban, but in 1950 it was only 40 per cent greater.[1] It is, indeed, a matter of common observation that many postwar urban families are composed of four, even five or more, children, compared with the two or three which characterized city families of a generation ago. This increase in size of urban and other nonfarm families is especially marked in the suburban fringe, areas occupied very

Table 15. Comparison of Number of Children under 5 per 1,000 Minnesota and U.S. Women 15 to 44, 1920 to 1950, by Residence

	1950		1940		1930		1920	
Residence	U.S.	Minn.	U.S.	Minn.	U.S.	Minn.	U.S.	Minn.
Urban*	412	458	257	272	315	302	381	375
Rural nonfarm...	560	607	400	393	471	423	527	502
Rural farm......	594	648	484	491	545	529	612	611
Total population .	742	527	329	352	391	387	467	474

Source: *United States Census of Population* for 1950 and 1940.
*Old urban definition (population in incorporated places of 2,500 or more).

largely by young families begun at the end of World War II. The number of children per woman tends to be larger in Minnesota than in the United States as a whole. There was a marked decline in both Minnesota and the nation from 1920 to 1940, but a sharp rise to 1950.

The head of the family. The farm family in Minnesota is more likely than the nonfarm to consist of husband, wife, and children. Also, it is more likely than others to have a male head. Whatever future conditions may justify changes in the composition of the family, farm life in the past has not been easy for the widowed husband or wife. When the husband dies, the wife will in many cases dispose of the farm and take up life in town or city. Farm life calls for the married pair: it is not so easy to get along when one of them is missing. Note the small percentage of female heads in the farm group as shown in Table 16.

While the proportion of husband-wife families in the farm group is larger than in the urban, it is not quite so large as that in the rural nonfarm. One explanation for this is the much larger proportion of village

[1] Birth rates are not reported by rural farm, rural nonfarm, and urban in the way the Bureau of the Census uses these categories. Nevertheless, it is possible to get an approximation of rural and urban comparisons. During the decade of the 1940's there was no marked difference in rates between the two categories. See *Migration in Minnesota 1940–1950*, Minnesota Agricultural Experiment Station Bulletin 422 (January, 1954).

couples in the age group 65 and over.[2] The much higher percentage of families in the farm group with "other male head" deserves a comment. While no information is available on the specific characteristics of this group, it is safe to say that a goodly number of these heads are bachelors. A not infrequent combination on Minnesota farms is a bachelor farmer with perhaps a widowed mother or a spinster sister keeping house for him. Some other male heads no doubt were widowers, with children or without. In a survey of seventy-one families in northwestern Minnesota in 1950, James H. Copp reported five widowers, two bachelors, and an

Table 16. Rural and Urban Minnesota Families by Type of Head, 1950

Residence	Husband No.	%	Other Male No.	%	Female No.	%	Total
Urban	365,732	87.8	12,602	3.6	38,174	9.2	416,508
Rural nonfarm	141,608	89.5	6,140	3.9	11,174	7.0	158,922
Rural farm	156,564	89.3	12,876	7.3	5,896	3.4	175,336
Total	663,904	88.4	31,618	4.2	55,244	7.4	750,766

Source: *U.S. Census of Population: 1950*, "Characteristics of Families," Table 34.

uncle-and-nephew combination. This makes a total of eight families with what the census might call "other male head," or more than one in ten of the total.[3] Although this is a small sample of rural Minnesota, it is suggestive of the explanation of the relatively large proportion of farm families other than the husband-wife type with a male head.

Size of households. It is common knowledge that the family has been growing smaller for many years. The census statistics are not very useful in demonstrating this because of the variations in methods of reporting: usually households are the units used instead of families. But one way of estimating family size is simply to divide the number of families, or households, into the total population and into each segment, urban, rural nonfarm, and rural farm. This procedure produces the results shown in Table 17.

This method does not take into account the fact that there are several thousand people who do not live as members of families, but it does serve

[2] This is shown in the Bureau of the Census report on "Characteristics of Families." While only 9.5 per cent of the male heads were 65 and over in the farm group, there were 15.7 per cent in this category in the nonfarm.

[3] James H. Copp, "Rosewood Study — Preliminary Data," unpublished manuscript in files of the Department of Rural Sociology, University of Minnesota.

61

to facilitate comparisons of the groups. The average size of the family has declined from 1930 to 1950, as might be expected. The pattern in Minnesota is similar to that of the nation, except that in 1930 the urban Minnesota family was slightly larger than the rural nonfarm family. While there was no difference between these groups nationally, Minnesota's averages are almost identical with those for the United States in each segment of the population.

Another source of information about size of family is one we have already used in this chapter, namely the census data on age and sex. These data can be used to calculate the number of children under 5 per 1,000 women in the childbearing years. Douglas G. Marshall used this method in comparing trends since 1875 of the fertility ratios in selected townships of the state representing various ethnic-religious groups. The conclusion was that there was a decline in all five townships (Anglo-American, Swedish, Norwegian, German Catholic, and German Lutheran), but some declined more than others. From 1875 to 1940 the German Lutheran declined most, nearly 65 per cent; the German Catholic, 40 per cent; Norwegian, 58 per cent; Swedish, 35 per cent; and Anglo-American, 22 per cent. However, the last three groups were considerably lower on the index in 1875 than were the two German townships, both of which had ratios of nearly 900 children per 1,000 women. This ratio was compared with around 650 for the Norwegian and Swedish, and only 450 for the Anglo-American. The study showed definitely the influence of religion on the German group, since one German township was Catholic and the other Lutheran, although generalizations could not be made on a broader scale from these small samples.[4]

Marriage Patterns

Finding marriage partners. I have already mentioned the disparity in the numbers of men and women 15 to 24 years of age on the farm — with a large surplus of men in the farm population. Since girls have obviously left in larger numbers than boys, the question inevitably arises as to where farm boys find their wives. On this matter one can only make some logical observations. The first is that now that more farm boys are going to high school the prospects for becoming acquainted with girls is much better than it was a few years ago. The second is that in spite of what the census

[4] Douglas G. Marshall, "Farm Family Size in Minnesota is Falling," *Minnesota Farm and Home Science*, Vol. VII, No. 1 (October, 1949) pp. 14–15.

shows regarding the high ratio of men in farm country, the probability is that the girls have not gone very far, they are probably working in the nearby village, town, or city. This is not, of course, true of all the girls; some have gone farther from home.

Propinquity has been found in many studies to be important in determining the choice of marriage partners. To find out what effect propinquity might have in the choices of couples in rural Minnesota, a study was made of the addresses of brides and grooms as reported on

Table 17. Comparison of the Average Number of Persons per Family or Household in Minnesota and in the United States, 1930 and 1950

Residence	1950		1930	
	U.S.	Minn.	U.S.	Minn.
All groups...............	3.38	3.40	4.1	4.2
Urban	3.24	3.21	4.0	4.1
Rural nonfarm............	3.45	3.29	4.0	3.8
Rural farm	3.98	4.00	4.6	4.7

Source: *U.S. Census of Population* for 1930 and 1950. The data for 1930 refer to families, those for 1950 to households.

marriage license applications from 1929 to 1939 in Carver and Scott Counties. Propinquity zones as developed by McClusky and Zander[5] in Michigan were used as follows: Group A consisted of those couples who gave the same post-office address within the county; Group B, gave different addresses within the county; in Group C, one member gave an address within the county and the other gave an address not more than 50 miles away; in Group D, one member gave an address within the county and the other gave an address more than 50 miles away.

For Scott County, Group A contained 41.4 per cent; Group B, 23.5 per cent; Group C, 28.2 per cent; and Group D, 6.9 per cent. For Carver County the respective percentages for the four groups were 36.2, 23.4, 33.5, and 6.9. It is obvious, and not unexpected, that the majority of the couples were from the same county and that in only a small fraction of the cases was one of the pair from more than 50 miles away.[6]

Ethnic and religious considerations. I have already shown (Chapter

[5] Howard Y. McClusky and Alvin Zander, "Residential Propinquity and Marriage in Branch County, Michigan," *Social Forces*, Vol. 19 (October, 1940) pp. 79–81.

[6] Donald Mitchell, "Residential Propinquity and Marriage in Carver and Scott Counties, Minnesota," *Social Forces*, Vol. 20, No. 2 (December, 1941) pp. 256–259.

III) that there is a marked tendency for persons to choose their marriage partners from their own ethnic background. There is no need to elaborate on this. It needs only to be mentioned that religious background also exerts a powerful influence on the choice. Or perhaps it is merely that persons who belong to the same church have an opportunity to meet and form friendships which mature into marriage. It is also a fact that religious denominations in the past have followed ethnic lines to a marked degree, so that the two factors often operate as one.

Marriage and divorce rates. Unfortunately it is not possible to compare rural and urban areas on rates of marriage and divorce, but statistics are available for the total population of the state going back to 1937. Figure 9 shows the extraordinary increase in Minnesota marriages

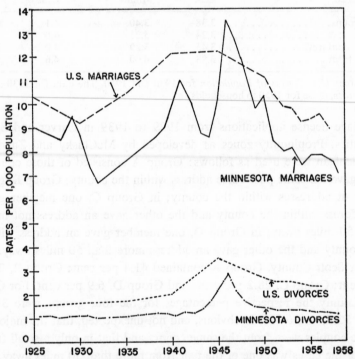

Figure 9. Number of Marriage Licenses Issued and Divorces Granted per Thousand Population in Minnesota and in the United States, 1925 to 1958 (Source: Minnesota Department of Health, Division of Vital Statistics, and *Statistical Abstract of the United States*, 1958, Table 56)

in the years immediately following the war, after which a decline began which continued to 1956. The rise in 1950 compared with 1949 was probably due to the Korean War. The decline after 1950 was the result of the decline in population of marriageable age already referred to in this chapter. Potential candidates for matrimony in the 1950's were born in the low birth-rate years of the 1930's. The period of high marriage rates was also one of high divorce rates, which hit the highest point in 1946. Since that year the decline has been marked and continuous. The number of divorces reported for Minnesota in 1956 was 3,948, with 24,604 marriages, or about one divorce for every six marriages. Only thirteen states had a lower ratio of divorces to marriages.

Divorce rates have long been regarded as an index of the stability or instability of the family. During the war these rates became so high as to inspire much discussion of possible causes and remedies. One attempted remedy over the years has been the introduction into high school and college curriculums of courses in family life, preparation for marriage, and the like. The Agricultural Extension Services in various states have responded by employing specialists in family relations. In part these developments are prompted by the belief that marriages may be made more stable and enduring if young people are given some premarital instruction about what to expect in marriage, what problems may arise, and how such problems may be handled. But in large measure these steps have also been taken in response to the expressed or implied need of parents to know better how to rear their children in order that they may be well-adjusted and prepared to meet the conditions and responsibilities of life in the modern world.

In the face of the widespread concern over the future of the family as an institution, and over the problems of rearing children in a world which has grown so much more complex than that of a generation ago, it is pertinent to review the results of some research carried on at Minnesota Agricultural Experiment Station on attitudes toward the family.

Children's Adjustment

Persistence of children's attitudes toward the family. In 1939 a scale for the measurement of morale which included a section devoted to attitudes toward the family was submitted to juniors and seniors of the Mora High School; in 1952 the same instrument was administered to the same

65

classes in that school.[7] The hypothesis was that changes in attitudes toward the family would have occurred in the thirteen-year interval because of the generally accepted decline in family solidarity as reflected in the high divorce rate, in the increased use of family counseling agencies, and in such developments as the reported rise in juvenile delinquency. Also it was supposed that the decline of primary group contacts, including the break-up of neighborhoods and the growth of anonymity, along with the improvement in economic conditions since 1939, might operate either to make the family mean more to the individual or perhaps less. In any case, it was assumed that there would be some change in the attitudes of young people and that these changes would be reflected in the scores on the scale.

The hypothesis that there have been changes in attitudes toward specific family relations between 1939 and 1952 was not borne out by the data with the methods used. Total family adjustment, the feeling that parents expect too much from their children, agreement between parents and children on ideals, and the view of home as a pleasant place, had not changed among the juniors and seniors of Mora High School. The sense of obligation to the family had increased somewhat during the period, but the differences were not statistically significant. There was a suggestion of somewhat more intimacy in the 1952 family than in the earlier group. Again this was not statistically significant.

Since more boys were attending school in 1952 than in 1939, a special test was made to ascertain what effect this larger proportion of boys might have on the result — in other words, the sex factor was controlled. The result was similar to that for the total group. The same or similar results were obtained when the groups were analyzed by occupation — farm and nonfarm. There was no difference in the attitudes of either group. Thus it was concluded that this study gives no support to the hypothesis that present-day young people have changed in family adjustment or in their attitudes toward specific family relations from the group tested in 1939.[8]

Comparative personality adjustment of children from rural and urban homes. If the farm environment is the ideal one in which to rear children,

[7] The scale was developed and standardized by Edward A. Rundquist and Raymond F. Sletto. See their *Personality in the Depression* (Minneapolis: University of Minnesota Press, 1936).

[8] See Charles E. Ramsey and Lowry Nelson, "Change in Attitudes Towards Family Relations," *American Sociological Review*, Vol. 21, No. 5 (October, 1956), pp. 605–609.

the proposition should be verifiable by such measurements of personality as are available to the researcher.[9] In applying the California Test to rural and urban children in the third and sixth grades in an Ohio county, A. R. Mangus concluded that farm children scored higher on the test than either city or small-town children. Teachers' ratings of "normal, healthy, wholesome" personalities were also more favorable for farm children.[10] Ivan Nye found the adjustment between farm high school boys and their parents to be generally poorer than that reported by urban, suburban, or town boys.[11]

The results of the Ohio survey were in line with the traditional expectations; those of Michigan were not. However, only grade school children were studied in Ohio and only high school boys in Michigan. On the assumption that a better comparison could perhaps be made if samples were drawn from the same state and preferably from the same school system, a project was organized at the Minnesota Agricultural Experiment Station which called for the administration in 1954 of tests to children in the third, seventh, and eleventh grades in five small-city school systems.[12] The cooperating school systems were those of Grand Rapids, Detroit Lakes, Thief River Falls, Pipestone, and Waseca. About 1,800 children filled out the schedules. Of these, 416 lived on farms, 438 were classified as rural nonfarm, and the remaining 981 lived in the five cities, which have populations of around 6,000.

There were no significant differences between farm and city children on personality adjustment as measured by the California Test and the Minnesota Scale of Child Adjustment. Third-grade farm boys scored slightly lower than those from the city on the latter scale, but the difference was not statistically significant. In short, it could not be said on the bases of these data that farm children were any better — or any worse — adjusted than city children. What is important, however, is that

[9] A number of such measuring devices have been developed and standardized on large populations. Among them are the California Test of Personality, and the Minnesota Scale of Child Adjustment.

[10] A. R. Mangus, "Personality Adjustment of Rural and Urban Children," *American Sociological Review*, Vol. 13, No. 5 (October, 1948), pp. 566–575.

[11] Ivan Nye, "Adolescent-Parent Adjustment — Rurality as a Variable," *Rural Sociology*, Vol. 15, No. 4 (December, 1950), pp. 334–339.

[12] The project, under the direction of Marvin J. Taves, was supported by a grant from the Louis and Maud Hill Family Foundation of St. Paul. This study is continuing. In 1958 schedules were obtained from the same school systems from pupils in grades 7 and 11 (3 and 7 in the 1954 study) thus making possible a measure of change over time.

the results did not establish farm children as *better* adjusted — as the traditional notion would imply.

Comparative adjustment of students at consolidated and nonconsolidated schools. In one of the five school systems, the Grand Rapids system, it was possible to make a comparison between the adjustment scores of children from the open country who attend consolidated and nonconsolidated schools. Schedules were obtained from 186 third, seventh, and eleventh graders who were attending schools in the open country, and 185 in the same grades who were attending the consolidated schools in Grand Rapids. All the children in both cases lived in the open country, and they were from both farm and nonfarm families. Of the nonconsolidated schools four were near and one in villages of less than 500 population. All schools, however, were part of and administered by the consolidated district of Grand Rapids. For convenience the two groups of children will be referred to as "consolidated" (those attending school in the city of Grand Rapids) and "nonconsolidated."

The findings support the thesis that personality adjustment is better among those who attend the consolidated schools. That is, on the average, those in all three grades who are transported to the Grand Rapids schools score higher than those who attend the five schools in the adjacent area. The open country, the little schoolhouse, the simpler life of the country, and all such familiar features so often associated with the "ideal" life for the family, did not show to advantage in the comparisons. In fact, the advantages were nearly all in favor of attending school in the city. While this may be an argument for consolidating schools, it is not to be regarded as a basis for generalization to other geographical areas. The results, however, should lead to caution in making unsupported generalizations about the superiority of the country as an environment for the family.[13]

Much concern has been expressed over the years about the difficulties of rearing children in the cities. Indeed, nobody can deny that the problems are serious. The shortage or absence of supervised play areas, the

[13] For detailed information see Mary R. Bonwell, "A Study of Personality Adjustment of Rural Children Attending Rural Schools and Rural Children Attending Urban Schools in the Grand Rapids, Minnesota Consolidated School District", unpublished M.A. thesis, University of Minnesota, December 1956. Also Marvin J. Taves, "Personality Adjustment of Rural Children Attending Consolidated and Nonconsolidated Schools," manuscript in Rural Sociology Department, University of Minnesota.

difficulty of finding useful employment appropriate for children, and many housing problems are apparent to anyone. Yet the country is not all sweetness and light as a family environment: for one thing, families from the city who move to the country to find space for the children are without the companionship of the father throughout much of the week. It is true, though, that farm boys and girls do not lack for space in which to play or parents close at hand to keep an eye on them. Then, too, there are small chores on the farm or in the home which can be assigned to children of practically all ages. Common sense suggests that these facts are important; but their virtue in producing superior personalities is not at all easy to demonstrate.

Farm families, like urban, are faced with many problems which are difficult to solve. Standards of living, which in the past were not so high as those of the city, have now risen so that farm children as they grow older are bound to put pressure on their parents for better housing and other things formerly not considered essential. Parents, too, under the stimuli of urban centers reaching them via radio, metropolitan newspapers, and the slick journals, are experiencing wants they formerly did not have.

The new wants arising from the bombardment of stimuli from the outside clamor for satisfaction. Tensions result when satisfaction lags too far behind fulfillment. The farm family has always been regarded as more stable and happier than the family in an urban environment, but there is growing evidence that the differences are not very great. The urban family, after all, has now had several generations in which to work out adaptations to the strange urban world. The farm family is now being subjected to the influences that once made life so difficult for urbanites. Family life in rural Minnesota is faced with the necessity of adapting to the urban-industrial world, not only economically, which is apparent to all, but also socially and psychologically. The need for research on the family engaged in farming is very great. What has been referred to in this chapter is but a meager beginning. This will be further evident when we view in the following chapter the vast changes which have come and are coming in the level of living.

v The Reach and the Grasp

ONLY a few years ago the phrase "standard of living" was universally used to designate the mode of life of the family, including such things as income, housing, and expenditures for various items necessary for the satisfaction of wants. Today a distinction is made between *level* and *standard* of living. The logic of this distinction is that standard carries the meaning and connotation of a goal, an ideal, an end to work toward. The standard of living, therefore, represents the total of the wants of a given person, family, or group, and as such it covers not only what has been attained but also desires that go beyond what can immediately be satisfied. The level of living, on the other hand, represents the degree to which the wants, desires, and goals represented by the standard are satisfied.

There is in most modern societies a considerable gap between the standard and the level, with the standard considerably higher than the level actually attained. This gap is sometimes referred to as an area of frustration. The gap is the incentive to strive for ever-increasing satisfaction of wants. As Robert Browning phrased it in "Andrea del Sarto," "a man's reach should exceed his grasp, / Or what's a heaven for?"

Measuring the Level of Living

There are several ways in which students have sought to measure the level of living. Studies of family budgets in Europe during the nineteenth century by such people as Frederic Le Play (1806–1882) and Ernst Engel (1821–1896) stimulated similar studies in the United States during the early twentieth century. Many studies of farm families were con-

70

ducted in several states during the 1920's.[1] Among the more significant of these were those carried on by Carle C. Zimmerman, rural sociologist of the Minnesota Agricultural Experiment Station, who not only described the way of life of farm families at different income levels, but also made comparisons between the mode of living and the utilization of income of village, town, and city families.[2]

Another method designed to measure the socio-economic level of an individual family is the socio-economic status scale. One of the earliest measuring instruments of this type was developed by F. Stuart Chapin, now professor emeritus of sociology at the University of Minnesota. His scale was based on the numerical scores assigned to items that characterize the manner of life of a family, including material possessions, income, and such nonmaterial items as the educational level of the people and their participation in the community.[3]

The Chapin scale was developed on the basis of urban investigations, but a modification of it was produced by William H. Sewell, using Oklahoma farm families.[4] The Sewell scale has been used widely through-

[1] Perhaps the earliest systematic study of farm families was made by E. L. Kirkpatrick, *The Standard of Life in a Typical Section of Diversified Farming*, Ithaca, New York: Cornell University Agricultural Experiment Station Bulletin No. 423 (July, 1923). Later, Kirkpatrick made studies of 2,886 farm families in eleven states and published a report, *The Farmer's Standard of Living*, United States Department of Agriculture Bulletin No. 1466, 1926. Finally, he brought together the results of these and other studies in a book, *The Farmer's Standard of Living* (New York: Century Company, 1929).

[2] Zimmerman was responsible for major studies of income and expenditures of Minnesota farm, village, town and city families. The studies were published under the following titles by the Minnesota Agricultural Experiment Station (with John D. Black) *Factors Affecting the Expenditures of the Farm Family Incomes in Minnesota*, Bulletin 246 (July, 1928); *How Minnesota Farm Family Incomes are Spent* (with John D. Black), Bulletin No. 234 (June, 1927); *Incomes and Expenditures of Village and Town Families in Minnesota*, Bulletin No. 253 (March, 1929); *Incomes and Expenditures of Minnesota Farm and City Families, 1927–28*, Bulletin No. 255 (June, 1929).

[3] F. Stuart Chapin, *The Measurement of Social Status* (Minneapolis: University of Minnesota Press, 1933). He defined socio-economic status as ". . . the position an individual or family occupies with reference to the prevailing average standards of cultural possessions, effective income, material possessions, and participation in the group activities of the community."

[4] William H. Sewell, *The Construction and Standardization of a Scale for the Measurement of the Socio-Economic Status of Oklahoma Farm Families*, Oklahoma Agricultural Experiment Station Technical Bulletin No. 9 (April, 1940). (In its essentials this was his Ph.D. dissertation at the University of Minnesota.) The abbreviated form of this scale was published in 1943. See "A Short Form of the Farm Family Socio-Economic Status Scale," *Rural Sociology*, Vol. 8, No. 2 (June, 1943) pp. 161–170.

71

out the United States and in Minnesota, because the results not only correlate highly with those of the more elaborate budgetary studies, but it is simple to administer and requires no more than a few minutes to complete. Also it provides a numerical score which facilitates statistical analysis in connection with other factors that may be under investigation.

The simplest device of all for providing a general level of living index is one developed by Margaret J. Hagood of the United States Department of Agriculture. This is called the farm-operator family level-of-living index. It has been calculated for every county and state in the United States. The components of the index are (a) the proportion of all farm homes in the county that are equipped with electricity, (b) the proportion that have telephones, (c) the proportion that have an automobile, and (d) the average value of farm products for the county. The numerical score for each county is based on the average of all farm families of that county and may not characterize any particular family. This index has the very great advantage of permitting comparisons among counties and areas of a given state as well as among states and regions of the United States.

Since the Census of Agriculture is taken by the United States Bureau of the Census every five years, it is also possible to use this index to measure change [5] in the level of living of families over a period of time. For example, the average farm operator's level of living for the state of Minnesota in 1945 was 129, with the United States' level equal to 100. The Minnesota index in 1950 was 151, and in 1954, 163. Each of the 87 counties from 1945 to 1950 increased its index, while from 1950 to 1954 only 80 of the counties showed an increase, with two counties remaining the same and five declining. The variation in the index by counties is shown in Figure 10.

Measuring Satisfaction with Family Living

It is one thing to enumerate the farm homes of the state which have various characteristics; it is quite a different thing to find out how the people who live in these homes feel about their way of life. In an effort to get an expression from a sample of farm housewives and a comparable

[5] The latest publication on these indexes is Margaret Jarman Hagood, Gladys K. Bowles, and Robert R. Mount, "Farm-Operator Family Level of Living Indexes for the Counties of the United States, 1945, 1950 and 1954," United States Department of Agriculture, Statistical Bulletin No. 204 (March, 1957).

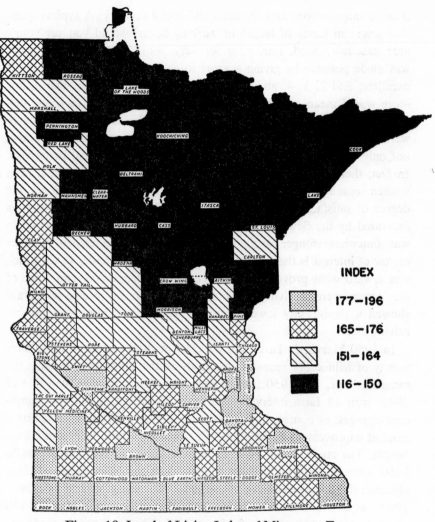

INDEX

▨ (dotted)	177—196
▨ (crosshatch)	165—176
▨ (diagonal)	151—164
■ (solid)	116—150

Figure 10. Level of Living Index of Minnesota Farm
Operators by County and Rank

sample of village housewives about various aspects of their lives, a survey was undertaken in Isanti County in 1940. The random samples consisted of sixty farm and fifty-two village housewives. Each woman was asked to indicate her feelings or judgment on seventy-one items dealing with food, clothing, educational opportunities, household conveniences, house and yard, health, recreation, social participation, working condi-

73

tions, transportation, and financial and social security. A typical question was: "in terms of length of working hours, would you say your's are: excellent, good, fair, poor, or very poor?"[6] A numerical score was made possible by giving a value to each of these responses: 1 for excellent, and 2, 3, 4, and 5 in ascending order for the others. A low score would mean a high degree of satisfaction, and a high score, dissatisfaction. The main conclusion of this study was that farm women were more dissatisfied with their conditions than were village women, not only on the average of all items, but on the individual items also. In fact, there was not a single item of the seventy-one on which farm women scored as satisfied as village women. As one might expect, the degree of satisfaction tended to increase with socio-economic status as measured by the Sewell Socio-Economic Status Scale. The relationship was somewhat stronger for the village than for the farm women. Another matter of interest is the time at which the study was made, 1940, which was toward what proved to be the end of the depression, and some of the farmers were receiving public aid. Those who did receive public aid showed a significantly lower degree of satisfaction than those not receiving aid.

In 1950 Marvin J. Taves and his class in rural sociology at the University of Minnesota repeated this study in the same county, using the same methods. The 1950 farm sample was slightly smaller than that of 1940, with 48 farm interviews but only 35 village interviews. Significant changes, of course, had taken place during the 1940's, including a marked improvement in the economic situation of both farm and village people. The study, however, revealed the same difference in scores in 1950 between farm and village women, with the latter more satisfied, although the differences were not so great. The score of farm women in 1940 was 2.89 and in 1950, 2.14; for village women in 1940 and 1950 respectively, the scores were 2.30 and 1.91. The farm people made the more significant gain, but still not enough to overcome the village lead.

There was also a difference in the items in the scale with which the women were most dissatisfied. In 1940 items causing greatest dissatisfaction from high to low were, in order: savings, bathrooms, vacations, sewage disposal systems, livingroom furniture, travel, hours of work, old age care prospects, strenuousness of work, and refrigerators. In 1950

[6] See Edgar C. McVoy and Lowry Nelson, *Satisfactions in Living: Farm vs. Village*, Minnesota Agricultural Experiment Station Bulletin No. 370 (June, 1943).

74

the comparable causes of most dissatisfaction were in order of rank: children's job prospects, savings, telephones, lawn, sewage disposal system, livingroom furniture, hours of work, recreation facilities for self, house, public library books, and books in the home.[7]

Changes in Farmers' Material Existence

Over the years since the original settlement of Minnesota, farm families have occupied houses of widely varying kinds and degrees of what might be termed adequacy. Early settlers faced with the urgent need of immediate shelter, constructed houses of the simplest kind and of the least costly material. "Least costly" usually meant that such houses could be built from materials at hand — trees, sod, or brick — about the only outlay for which would be sweat and toil. Where timber was available log houses were the rule; while on the prairie sod was used. Such primitive abodes would be vacated and used for purposes other than family living or torn down as soon as more adequate houses could be constructed.

Pioneer houses were heated with stoves or fireplaces and lighted with kerosene lamps, candles, or a simple oil wick. Wood, of which there was an abundance in most areas of the state except the plains, was the main fuel. However, coal, brought into the state by Mississippi River barge, Great Lakes ship, and railroad, gradually came to be predominant. In a study of 226 farm families made in the summer of 1928, Carle C. Zimmerman had this to say: "The homes were heated by common stoves, hard-coal heaters and parlor furnaces, pipeless furnaces, and full central heating plants. The three major types were stoves, partial central heating plants (pipeless furnaces), and full central heating plants." [8] His survey showed that 32.8 per cent of the houses had full central heating plants, a higher percentage than for the entire state in 1940, when only 19 per cent of the farm homes had central heating. The farms surveyed by Zimmerman were doubtless above average. They were located within the trading areas of two fairly large centers, one of 15,000 persons, the other of 50,000, as of 1920.

An earlier study, made in the fall of 1925 by Zimmerman, covered 357 farm families in seven counties and was designed to be representa-

[7] Marvin J. Taves, "Farm Versus Village Living: A Decade of Change," *Rural Sociology*, Vol. 17, No. 1 (March, 1952) pp. 47–55.

[8] Carle C. Zimmerman, *Incomes and Expenditures of Minnesota Farm and City Families, 1927–28*," Minnesota Agricultural Experiment Station Bulletin No. 255 (June, 1929) pp. 43 ff.

tive of the state as a whole.[9] He reported that 29.5 per cent of the houses had central heating, some of which was the "pipeless kind." A large proportion of houses with central heating used stoves as supplementary heating. Lighting was mainly by kerosene, exclusively so in 53 per cent of the homes, and in conjunction with gasoline lamps in 24 per cent. Acetylene lighting systems were found in 5 per cent of the homes, and electricity in 18 per cent. Of the last about one third of the houses drew power from private or individual plants, the rest from public lines. It might be added that drinking water for these families came from wells outside the house in the majority of cases, with 33 per cent having pumps in the kitchens, drawing water from cisterns.

In the century which stretches from the sod and log houses to the present day, the housing and other conveniences of farm families have steadily improved. Changes have been wrought with great rapidity, particularly since 1940. The prosperity which came to American farmers with the outbreak of World War II and which continued in the postwar years is undoubtedly the most remarkable in the history of American agriculture. It is true that during the second decade of the century when another war was in progress and up until the collapse of 1920, agriculture was very prosperous. However, the newly won prosperity of that period induced farmers to invest their surplus in land, with the result that prices of land rose to unprecedented levels. Then when the crash came farmers not only lost their equities, but the decline was so great as to reduce the value of the land far below the amount of the mortgage which it bore.

The same mistake of investing in land the surplus cash gained from wartime prices was not repeated after World War II. The memory of what had happened earlier was still fresh enough in the minds of American farmers, and certainly in the minds of those responsible for guiding agricultural policy, that the idea of investing their new gains in improving the living conditions of their families was encouraged.[10]

Moreover, the creation of the Rural Electrification Administration in 1935 made available to farm people electricity from central generating plants. While wartime scarcities of materials limited the rate at which electrification could take place, some progress was made, and in the

[9] Carle C. Zimmerman, *How Minnesota Farm Family Incomes are Spent*, Minnesota Agricultural Experiment Station Bulletin No. 234 (June, 1927) p. 20.

[10] See Lowry Nelson, *Can Farmers Afford to Live Better?* Washington, D.C.: National Planning Association, Planning Pamphlets, No. 65, 1948.

period after the war it was greatly accelerated. Whereas only 30 per cent of farms were equipped with electricity in 1940, the percentage had risen to 82 per cent by 1950, and by 1955 was almost 100 per cent.

The availability of electricity has undoubtedly contributed to the rise in the number of houses with running water, since it makes automatic water systems possible. Only 12 per cent of farm homes in 1940 reported running water, while by 1950 there had been practically a fourfold increase to 47 per cent. Although this is still far below the rate for town and city families, the increase is going on so rapidly that perhaps practically all farm homes will have running water within the next ten or fifteen years. Running water means that houses can have indoor flush toilets and otherwise fully equipped bathrooms. Electricity on a reliable service basis also makes possible the use of the numerous appliances so common in town and city homes.

Vernon Davies, using the Housing Census data for 1940, compared Minnesota farm dwelling units with those of the other states of the union and with the national average. In comparing Minnesota on the 11 items with the United States average (Table 18), he found the state falling

Table 18. Comparison of Minnesota Farms with United States Average on Housing and Conveniences, 1940 and 1950

	1940		1950	
	Minn.	U.S.	Minn.	U.S.
Housing				
Median no. of rooms.........	5.9	4.7	6.1	5.1
No. persons per dwelling......	4.3	4.3	4.0	4.0
1.51 or more persons per room.	8.9%	16.0%	4.2%	10.2%
House built before 1930......	*	*	76.6%	68.3%
House built since 1930.......	*	*	31.7%	23.4%
Need major repairs..........	27.0%	34%	8.3%	19.5%
Convenience				
Electric lights..............	30.0%	31.3%	84.0%	80.0%
Mechanical refrigerator.......	9.6%	14.9%	67.5%	62.7%
Radio	85.3%	60.2%	82.8%	92.0%
Running water, hot and cold...	12.2%	17.8%	26.1%	28.5%
Flush toilet................	7.8%	11.2%	25.0%	27.7%
Private bath	7.7%	11.8%	24.8%	29.8%
Central heating.............	19.4%	10.1%	29.5%	18.1%

Source: Vernon Davies, *Farm Housing Needs,* Minnesota Agricultural Experiment Station Bulletin No. 393 (March, 1947), p. 20, and *U.S. Census of Housing 1950,* Vol. 1, Part 1.
*Essential comparisons shown in 1950 figures.

into the low position on 5 of them. The favorable percentage for central heating is a consequence of the cold climate. The state had a lower proportion of its homes provided with running water, flush toilet, and private bath.

Marked improvement in farm housing is revealed in the 1950 census. The proportion of houses in need of major repairs fell from 27 to 8.3 per cent; a much more favorable development than for the nation. Minnesota rose from an unfavorable to favorable position — compared with the nation — on percentages of homes with electric lights and mechanical refrigeration but still lagged on running water, private bath and flush toilet. Minnesota farm houses are also older on the average; 76.6 per cent, compared with 68.3 per cent for the nation, were built before 1930. It is not clear why this disparity in age should exist, although it may be the result of superior original construction because of the climate.

Some idea of what has been happening to farm housing since 1950 can be gained from the United States Census of Agriculture taken in the fall of 1954. The figures on household conveniences are not entirely comparable with those secured in the regular decennial Census of Housing, but they are sufficient to indicate trends. For example, the decennial Census of Housing for 1950 reports cold and hot running water in the house, while the agricultural census reports running water on the farm. Table 19 shows a comparison for various years from 1920 to 1954.

The steady growth in the possession of certain facilities by the farm families of Minnesota is obvious, but what is most noteworthy is the increase in electrification, running water, and possession of home freezers and television. The last two are relatively new and are generally dependent upon the availability of electrical current for their use. By con-

Table 19. Percentage of All Minnesota Farms with Specified
Conveniences, 1920–1954

Convenience	1920	1930	1940	1945	1950	1954	U.S. Avg., 1954
Telephone	62.0%	61.9%	44.6%	54.6%	59.9%	68.3%	48.8%
Electricity	7.6	12.6	30.3	50.5	84.1	94.1	93.0
Running water	6.4	12.5	12.1	20.5	56.5	57.1	58.8
Home freezer	...	...	...	...	16.4	38.5	32.2
Television	...	...	...	...	1.8	33.3	35.5

Source: *U.S. Census of Agriculture: 1954*, Vol. II, Chap. III, Table 5.

trast with its low rank in 1940, Minnesota in 1954 is very close to the national average on all of these items.

Possession of telephones has fluctuated rather widely over the years in Minnesota and the nation, reaching a low point in 1940, obviously as a result of the depression, and only approaching the percentages for 1920 and 1930 by 1950 or 1954. Apparently the telephone is one thing farm families will dispense with when times get hard. Recent legislation providing for loans from the REA for the development of local cooperative telephone companies, similar to those for electrification, have undoubtedly spurred the spread of this facility throughout the rural farm areas.

Nonmaterial Influences on the Level of Living

Thus far I have reported some of the pronounced changes in the living level of farm families as shown by housing and the possession of certain utilities. These are material things which, it must be pointed out, add to comfort and convenience but are not to be regarded as the most important values in life. It cannot be established, for example, that the pioneer families in their log and sod houses were any less happy than families today, although they might have been. They certainly were much less comfortable. But to say that what we have been considering as material conveniences are not the whole of life and living is not to say that they are to be denied to farm people. As much as their town and city cousins, farm people should be able to enjoy and use these facilities which modern technology has made possible.

Whether or not families obtain these conveniences depends first upon their wants and ideals. Money is necessary, of course, but there must be a felt need for the goods and services. There are many stories, partly legendary but sometimes true, to the effect that farmers provide better housing for their livestock than they do for their wives and children. The cows may have individual automatic drinking cups in their stalls while the housewife has to carry water from the pump near the barn. That such cases existed few informed observers can deny, but happily they are progressively more difficult to find. The fact that they ever did exist was often because of circumstances which made it more important to invest available capital in ways which would bring immediate increased profits than to invest it in what seemed to be unproductive housing facilities.

While it is not always the availability or the scarcity of funds that determines whether or not a family will improve its living conditions, money is decisive in most cases. So it must be recognized that the increased prosperity of farming since 1940 has made possible the improvements we have described above.

Along with the increased income must go the desire for the improvements. What the family members, particularly the husband and wife, think is important in life determines how they will spend their income. Are running water and a fully equipped bathroom important? Or would the money be better spent as part payment on the adjacent forty, or on some more cows, or on a new tractor? Such decisions must be made every day on the farms of the state. What influences them? There will be individual situations to consider, needs and resources of the farm versus the home, the education of the children, and many other competing wants. But along with the particular influences, there will be others at work: among these are the level of education of the husband and wife, the level of income, the social participation of both. High participators usually have a higher level of living; the higher the education, the higher the level of living tends to be; and the higher the income, the more likely that money will be spent on the farm home. Status considerations, in short, will have much to do with the consumption pattern of the family.

It might appropriately be asked whether the matters we have just discussed include all that is involved in the phrase level of living. How important, really, to satisfaction with life — to human happiness, if you please — are deep freezes, running water, modern plumbing, electricity, automobiles? Any rational person must answer that these are but incidentals to the good life. Many other things are much more important. High income, modern housing, the automobile, and all the technological gadgetry are important, but they are not the only things that concern people. By and large, the level of living encompasses schools, churches, highways, government, wholesome family life — in the sense of good relations among the members — recreation, and so on. The level of these nonmaterial matters is a truer measure of a civilization than the quantity and multiplicity of conveniences.

Some of these nonmaterial matters will be treated in a separate chapter. However, there is one of them that calls for a few observations and of which there will be no further discussion beyond what is said here:

this may be broadly comprehended under the term recreation. Recreation, like so many social problems, is both a personal and a public concern. Most people like to have and may insist upon freedom to choose what they do in their leisure hours. Any coercion would rob leisure of the spontaneity which is its essential quality. People want to be free to read when they feel like reading. They want to go fishing when they think they would enjoy fishing. They would like to be free to decide whether to play tennis on the public tennis courts, golf on the public golf course, or to swim at a properly maintained public bathing beach. If they like art, they want to visit the art gallery, and at a time they choose.

All such activities presuppose the availability of facilities, and availability assumes joint action with others to provide and support them. Even such an obviously individual activity as fishing cannot be available without public action to conserve the fish. A pleasure ride in the family car depends upon the availability of highways, and so on through a long list of recreational activities. Thus, it is clear that there must be community action — local, state, national — in order that certain kinds, perhaps most kinds, of recreation may be enjoyed.

Recreation assumes special importance in the contemporary world because of the technological revolution which has taken much of the burden of work off the individual, increased his productive power, and released to him more free time than he ever had before. Arguments against limiting the work-day, and the work-week, have held that workers would not know what to do with the time released, and that their idleness would make them vulnerable to the temptations of vice and crime. Though this may sound convincing to some, the evidence to support it would be very difficult to find. Nevertheless, between sheer loafing and vice or crime there is a wide gradation of behavior. This gradation results from the freedom of choice mentioned above, and, of course, the availability of resources.

With the remarkable increase in labor-saving equipment on the farms, people often ask how farmers and their families spend the leisure time released to them by these improvements. There have been few studies which might provide the answers, and this is a field where research is much needed.

In a dynamic society, the "reach" is always ahead of the "grasp." Minnesota is such a dynamic society. Always there are new wants, needs, aspirations which call for more goods and services. This constant multiplication of wants results in a concomitant rise in the levels of attainment. To some this process is progress; in any case it is social change. Progressively, Minnesotans are better housed, better fed, better able to communicate rapidly with others, and are better educated than were their parents and grandparents. How much formal education they have will be revealed in the chapter to follow.

VI There Shall Be Education in the Land

ESTABLISHING social life and institutions in a land that is being wrested from the wilderness calls for heroic effort. The pioneers who came to settle the land of Minnesota were motivated, quite naturally, by the prospect of improving their economic condition. But their aspirations went beyond the material. Many came from countries and communities where social life was well established and where opportunities for learning the basic arts of writing, reading, and ciphering were available even to the poor. Not all took advantage of these opportunities perhaps, but the literacy rates in Northern and Western Europe were relatively high for the time.

Think for a moment of the hazards which confronted the pioneers, not only the adults but the children as well. All were more or less subjected to the physical hazards of frontier life. Unfamiliar weather, unfriendly human beings or animals, and many other features of the new environment surrounded the newcomer with perils. Lawless refugees from older settlements sought the seclusion of the new area where normal facilities for control were lacking or inadequate.

There were nonphysical risks too, especially the danger that the first children of the frontier might have fewer cultural opportunities than the parents. This was especially true of education. Without extraordinary effort's being put forth, the children of the frontier might be less educated and represent a retrogression from the parental level.

The roots of this danger are apparent. New settlers found it necessary to do many tasks at once. First and foremost was physical survival,

83

above all breaking the ground to plant the seeds they brought with them — seeds to provide the hoped-for harvest to feed them and their animals through the winter. They had to have shelter also, a matter of extreme importance in the Upper Midwest, where winters are severe. Thus plowing, planting, building, and reaping were among the first tasks of the new settlers. Only as physical survival was assured were they able to devote time and effort to less urgent tasks.

These "less urgent" tasks were of vast importance. Among them was providing schools. Church services could be held in homes if need be, but teaching the young is less episodic and more formal. It was possible to impart the rudiments of an education at home, but parents so largely preoccupied with physical survival had but limited time available for teaching the young. Teaching calls for a person who can give it his full time.

Education, moreover, requires special facilities. While classes might be held in private homes, the earliest houses were scarcely adequate for such purposes. Special structures must be built. This required time, and the loss of time in school is one of the great hazards to the young. The situation was always complicated by the difficulty of getting teachers. In the history of the American frontier, in many cases if not most, one of the more literate laymen of the new settlement was called upon to teach the children.

The critical period is the first few years. As rapidly as soil was broken and planted and harvested in sufficient amounts to assure survival, more and more attention could be given to buildings. It was then that neighbors united their efforts to construct a school and agreed to contribute toward the teacher's salary. What was of greatest importance was the will to provide education. Where the aspirations of the parents are high, the schools are forthcoming.

Pioneer Schools

Fortunately for Minnesota, the early settlers were people with high aspirations. Says Merrill E. Jarchow:

. . . At first the log cabins were used as schoolhouses. Mrs. Gideon Pond, who came to Bloomington in the middle 1850's, often shared with other mothers the task of teaching the neighborhood children who gathered for lessons every morning around the kitchen table in her house. In another locality an observer saw twenty-four Norwegian children "studiously at work" in the attic of a log cabin. As population increased, schoolhouses were built. Mrs. Margaret R. Funk attended such a school in Mankato in the winter of 1853–54. "The schoolhouse was built by popular subscription," she wrote. "It was a log structure of one room, and in the middle of this room was a large, square, iron stove. The pupils sat around the room facing the four walls . . . I came from my home across the prairie, through the snow in the bitter cold of winter . . . The education the children received in those days had to be paid for either by their parents or by someone else who picked out a child and paid for his or her tuition.[1]

The late Warren H. Wilson comments in eloquent language on the devotion of the pioneer ("land farmer" to him) to education:

The farmers who out of a splendid idealism placed a schoolhouse at every cross-roads, on every hill-top, and in every mountain valley, exact a tribute of praise from their successors. The unit of measurement of the school district, on which this system was based, was the day's journey of a child six years of age. Two miles must be its longest radius. The generation who spanned this continent with the measure of an infant's pace, mapped the land into districts, erected houses at the centers, and employed teachers as masters of learning for these little states, were men of statesman-like power. The country school is a nobler monument of the land farmer than anything else . . .[2]

Another quotation seems to characterize well the founders of Minnesota, as it was presumed to characterize the people of Scotland. Sir James M. Barrie in his rectorial address at St. Andrews University on May 3, 1922, after referring to the four great universities of Scotland, proposed a fifth and greatest one as being "the poor, proud homes you come out of, which said so long ago: 'There shall be education in this land.' "

The first schools of a frontier community were usually provided on a voluntary basis, supported by private contributions from parents. Often these contributions were in the form of commodities; when cash was difficult to come by, the teacher accepted his pay in kind. Later when the state was organized and a constitution adopted, one of its articles provided for schools. Article VIII, Section 1, states: "The stability of a republican form of government depending mainly upon the intelli-

[1] Merrill E. Jarchow, *The Earth Brought Forth* (St. Paul: Minnesota Historical Society, 1949), p. 108.
[2] Warren H. Wilson, *The Evolution of the Country Community* (Boston: Pilgrim Press, 1912), p. 24.

gence of the people, it shall be the duty of the legislature to establish a general and uniform system of public education."

The device for implementing this constitutional mandate was the local school district. The state legislature set the conditions under which local citizens might ask for the creation of a district. This district had the authority to levy taxes for school purposes and to elect the trustees responsible for conducting the affairs of the district. These include the provision of schoolrooms and the employment of teachers. The county superintendent approves the teachers, who are expected to meet standards of training for certification set by the state. The state is made responsible under the federal constitution for the conduct of the educational system. The State Board of Education is entrusted with the general administration of state laws. It issues certificates to qualified teachers, gathers statistics on school population and enrollment, apportions and transmits state school aid to the districts, and in general keeps up the standards set by the state.

The local school district is the instrumentality by which rural people provided schooling through the grades. The typical school was one room, presided over by a teacher who taught all eight grades. In the course of time many of the local districts proved unnecessary because of dwindling or disappearing enrollment. The larger families of earlier years provided ample pupils to justify the operation of the schools originally created to serve them. But the decline in the size of the family since the turn of the century, plus the decline in total farm population, meant a decline in enrollment that became especially notable in the late 1930's and early 1940's. Thousands of school districts found it more convenient and economical to contract with a neighboring district to teach its one or two children; others decided to go out of existence entirely.

Until 1947 no orderly procedure was set up by the state legislature whereby local people might analyze their school district situation and vote on plans for reorganization. Under the statute adopted by the legislature, county survey committees, with counsel from the state Board of Education and especially with the aid of the special state Advisory Commission on School Reorganization, could study local problems and if necessary recommend to the voters a plan for reorganization. At that time there were 7,684 school districts in the state, 20 per cent of which had an enrollment of fewer than 10 pupils and 70 per cent of fewer

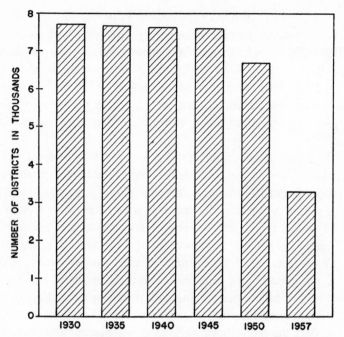

Figure 11. Change in Number of School Districts in
Minnesota, 1930 to 1957

than 19 pupils. Of the high schools, over a third had enrollments of fewer
than 100 and 8 per cent had fewer than 50 pupils.

By 1951 when the Advisory Commission on School Reorganization
made its second report to the legislature, 20 counties had voted against
and 63 for the creation of county survey committees. This report noted
a decline of nearly nine hundred districts since 1948, most of it attributa-
ble to the activities of the county survey committees.

The decline has continued through the years; and in 1957, ten years
after the legislature acted, the number of districts had declined to 3,298
(Figure 11). The dramatic shift at the county level is shown by Goodhue
County which declined from 155 districts in 1946 to 16 in 1958. And
among the 16 district, there were 4 which were not conducting school
during 1957 — 1958.[3]

[3] Lee Taylor, Marvin J. Taves, and Gordon Bultena, *Changing Goodhue County,
1946–1958*, Sociology of Rural Life Bulletin No. 1, Minnesota Agricultural Experiment Station (January, 1959).

Numbers Attending School

By the opening of the twentieth century Minnesota had succeeded in providing grade school education for practically all of its children. By 1910, of the age group 7–13 years, 92.6 per cent of the rural and 93.7 per cent of the urban were attending school. By 1950 the enrollment in this age group was around 97 per cent for both rural and urban. As far as grade school education is concerned, Minnesota has performed very well.

With high school education the situation is much different. In fact, up to 1950 Minnesota was consistently one of the lowest-ranking states in the proportion of its farm boys and girls 16–17 years of age who were attending school at the time the censuses were taken. I have often been asked the source of my data on school attendance. The answer is the United States Census of Population for the various years; the Bureau of the Census has asked the families in each enumeration to indicate which of the children are attending school. Since many persons were surprised to find Minnesota ranking so low among the states, there was naturally much concern as to the source of the information. In comparing states, only the native-born white of native parents were considered. This eliminated Negroes from the data, but also the native born of foreign or mixed parentage, and the foreign-born. Both of these groups were numerically important in Minnesota and adjoining states, and both had lower attendance records than the native-born of native white parents. The ranking of the states for 1930, 1940, and 1950 is shown in Table 20.

The low position of Minnesota in the attendance of farm young people is reflected in the proportion of the adult farm population 25 years of age or over with high school or college education. In the proportion of the farm population with any high school education, Minnesota ranked 43 in 1940 with 21.2 per cent; and 42 in 1950 with 27.6 per cent. The highest state in both years was Utah with 53.1 per cent in 1940 and 65.7 per cent in 1950. The lowest in 1940 was West Virginia with 12.3 per cent and in 1950 it was Kentucky with 18.7 per cent.

In 1940 only 0.7 per cent of Minnesota's adult farm population had four years of college or more, and in 1950 only 1.0 per cent. In both years its rank was 47; only Arkansas was below it. The highest state was Arizona with 7.0. Arkansas was the low state in both years with 0.6 per cent in 1940 and 0.9 per cent in 1950. The national averages for

Table 20. Ranks of States in Percentage of Native White Rural Farm Boys and Girls 16 and 17 Years Old Who Were Enrolled in School in 1930, 1940, and 1950

	Rank					Rank		
	1930	1940	1950			1930	1940	1950
Alabama	23	34	40		Nebraska	25	19	17
Arizona	16	25	46		Nevada	4	6	5
Arkansas	19	43	39		New Hampshire	14	16	23
California	2	3	7		New Jersey	34	24	18
Colorado	17	17	15		New Mexico	13	20	29
Connecticut	41	12	8		New York	27	13	22
Delaware	30	31	37		North Carolina	29	37	35
Florida	11	32	26		North Dakota	40	41	36
Georgia	37	42	47		Ohio	8	8	9
Idaho	5	5	4		Oklahoma	18	18	11
Illinois	32	28	21		Oregon	6	4	2
Indiana	9	11	14		Pennsylvania	44	30	28
Iowa	22	21	10		Rhode Island	45	27	34
Kansas	10	7	6		South Carolina	24	33	41
Kentucky	39	48	48		South Dakota	31	23	36
Louisiana	34	36	31		Tennessee	25	46	43
Maine	21	22	32		Texas	20	26	33
Maryland	46	45	42		Utah	1	1	1
Massachusetts	28	15	12		Vermont	33	38	38
Michigan	38	29	13		Virginia	36	39	44
Minnesota	47	40	24		Washington	3	2	3
Mississippi	7	14	19		West Virginia	41	47	45
Missouri	43	35	30		Wisconsin	48	44	25
Montana	15	10	16		Wyoming	12	9	20

Sources: *United States Census of Population* for 1930, 1940, and 1950. See also Lowry Nelson, *Education of the Farm Population of Minnesota*, Minnesota Agricultural Experiment Station Bulletin No. 347 (1944) and "Marked Progress Made by Minnesota in Rural Education" (mimeo) (November, 1953).

this category were for 1940, 1.5, and for 1950, 2.4 per cent. It is clear up to this point that Minnesota, while educating its farm children very extensively at the grade school level, falls short of the national average as far as their high school and college training are concerned.

Why Does Minnesota Rank So Low?

The data call for some explanation. Why should a state with a comparatively high per-capita wealth, which does so well with the elementary education of its children, not carry through on the upper levels? It has been widely implied that the wealth available to a state has something to do with its educational performance. On the assumption that wealth might be a factor at the county level, the high school attendance percentages of counties were ranked. This revealed the surprising fact that many poor agricultural counties ranked high, and many rich ones low. Having observed that the attendance of farm girls was somewhat better than the attendance of farm boys, 62.7 per cent and 43.9 per cent respectively, it was considered possible that the boys were being kept out of high school in greater proportions in the good counties because their work was needed on the farm. A further explanation was suggested: particular ethnic groups were prominent in some of the low-ranking counties, and they might be guided by Old World values regarding education. For example, in Germany it has been the custom to decide at the fifth-grade level whether the child is to go on and prepare for the university and a profession, or whether he is to go to a trade school or a school of agriculture. If the latter, the instruction is very practical for both boys and girls. It may be that some of the people of German, Polish, or Bohemian descent who live in Minnesota have adhered to the Old World standards more closely than have others.

Finally, since distance from a high school was found in an earlier study to be associated with attendance of farm boys and girls (see note under Table 20), it was assumed that the availability of transportation would be a factor. Statistical tests of the influence of the value of land and improvements per acre, enrollment in high schools having fewer than 100 pupils, the percentage of total farm males enrolled in the vocational-agricultural course in the high schools, and the cost of public transportation per pupil were also run. None of these four proved to be related to a significant degree, and attention was focused on the following four factors:

1. The index of cultural characteristics, derived from (a) the nationality background (especially German, Slavic, and southern European), (b) the intensity of enrollment in elementary parochial schools, and (c) the predominance of three religious groups: Missouri Lutheran Synod, Wisconsin Lutheran Synod, and Roman Catholic.

2. Labor requirements per farm, measured by the man-work unit defined as the work accomplished in a ten-hour day by one man working with average efficiency. Data came from the 1940 census and from the Farm Management Service of the Department of Agricultural Economics of the University of Minnesota.

3. Value of farm products per farm, as derived from the 1940 census.

4. Availability of bus transportation, using an index obtained by dividing the actual bus mileage by the improved road mileage in the county.[4]

The result of the statistical analysis shows that each of the four exerts a definite influence on attendance at high school. Ten of the lowest-ranking fourth of the counties on school attendance are in the highest ranking quarter of the counties on the culture index. That is to say, the greater the degree of dominance in the population of people of German, Slavic, or southern European background, the lower the high school attendance seems to be. (This ignores the parochial school enrollment and religious affiliation for purposes of brevity. These factors are closely tied to nationality.) Moreover, there are eight of these counties high on the culture index which are in the second lowest quarter of the school attendance counties. Only two of the high culture index counties are in the second highest fourth on attendance, and only two are in the top fourth. It must be pointed out that there are other counties that rank low in school attendance which do not have these cultural characteristics — which may safely be regarded as evidence that there are also other factors involved in low school attendance.

Turning now to the influence of labor requirements, we find that about twenty-five per cent of the variation in school attendance of farm boys can be accounted for by this. As Marshall and Peterson point out, there were five counties in the highest quarter on the basis of labor requirements which were in the lowest fourth on attendance. Six of the remaining counties with high labor requirements fall in the third quarter in school attendance, six are in the second, and five are in the first quartile on school attendance. Thus, the twenty-two counties which rank highest in labor requirements are quite evenly divided among the four quarters on school attendance.

As regards the value of farm products per farm in 1940, which is after all a fair measure of the financial ability of a county to send its farm boys to high school, the results are not in the expected direction. Of the twenty-three counties which ranked highest on this item, five were in the lowest fourth on school attendance, ten in the next to the lowest, and only four each in the first and second quartiles or the upper half on attendance.

[4] See Douglas Marshall and Milo J. Peterson, *Factors Associated with Variations in School Attendance of Minnesota Farm Boys,* published jointly by the Agricultural Experiment Station, the Graduate School, and the Bureau of Educational Research of the University of Minnesota (July, 1948). This report gives a full description of the operation involved in the statistical analysis.

91

Clearly, this factor is inversely related: the higher the value, the lower the school attendance. It is probably related to the other factor of labor requirements and both seem to operate in an unexpected manner.

The availability of bus transportation must be regarded as being itself an expression of the values of people with respect to education. If the aspiration for high school education for their children is strong enough, the parents will see that the children get to school. The results demonstrate once more the fact that this is not a matter of wealth as far as farm products sold is an index. Fifteen of the twenty-one counties with low index of bus availability are in the southern part of the state where high agricultural productivity prevails. Fourteen of them are in the lower half of the counties on school attendance and only seven in the upper half. Again, it must be said that other counties which rank low on attendance are better off with reference to transportation.

Marshall and Peterson conclude that while all these factors have proved to be related to school attendance, no one of them alone can be called responsible for low attendance in a particular county. Ethnic or cultural background appears definitely associated with low attendance in many counties. It may be that there is a persistence of Old World values in regard to the amount and kind of education a boy should have in order to be a successful farmer. Certainly, too, among the groups mentioned are to be found some of the most efficient and productive farmers of the state. Perhaps the kind of high school training available is not necessary for success on those farms. Tradition as handed down from father to son may serve well as a substitute for formal schooling. Farm labor requirements have in the past exerted an influence on school attendance, but it is not too much to expect that with the rate of mechanization and automation which has characterized agriculture since 1940, the need for keeping boys out of school for farm work will soon disappear. Finally, there should be no question about the ability of the state to provide whatever education it may decide is necessary or desirable. Some of the richest counties in the state, agriculturally, have low attendance and poor rating on availability of transportation.

It is not my purpose, nor has it been the purpose of the research carried on in this field at the Agricultural Experiment Station of the University of Minnesota, to praise or blame any person or group for supporting or not supporting high school education. It is not our purpose to say whether high school education, or college education, is necessary or desirable for the farm people of Minnesota. I think it is desirable and that it may become highly necessary for farm operators to have college training. But that is only my opinion. It is for the people of the state to decide what kind and how much education they should provide for the young.

Studies in Selected Communities

Although the analysis of census data by counties of the state revealed definite association between certain factors and the educational level, it was considered desirable to test certain hypotheses by interviewing people in four selected communities.

Two questions in the schedule designed to test favorableness toward education were (1) "What amount of education do you consider sufficient for your children?" and (2) "Check 'yes' or 'no' on each of the following statements: (a) Grade school with reading, writing, and arithmetic is good enough for farming, (b) High schools take the boys and girls away from the farm, (c) Schools should offer more subjects of vocational interest to agriculture, (d) Children of today need more education, (e) The farm boy can learn all he needs to know about farming from his father, and (f) Farming requires as much education as any other occupation."

A German Catholic community: St. Martin. One of these communities was St. Martin in Stearns County, composed of approximately a township of territory and inhabited by 145 families, all of whom are of German extraction and Roman Catholic. Of the 145 families, 109 live on farms, the rest in the village. Although the villagers of St. Martin are of the same ethnic-religious background as the farm people, they differ markedly from them in what they regard as sufficient education for their children (Table 21). Since, as we have noted earlier, it is the failure of farm youngsters to attend high school that brings Minnesota's rating down, it is significant that nearly half of the farm parents of St. Martin regard grade school as sufficient. None of them considers college necessary.

The responses to the second question (Table 22) indicate considerable confusion about education goals, on the part of the farm people particularly. For example, while 69 per cent voted grade school as sufficient training (item a), 63 per cent said "yes" to "Farming requires as much education as any other occupation" (item f). Also note that over half said "yes" to "The farm boy can learn all he needs to know about farm-

Table 21. The Responses of St. Martin Parents, Village and
Farm, Regarding Amount of Education Sufficient
for Children, 1951

Amount of Education	Combined Groups (N = 145)	Village (N = 36)	Farm (N = 109)
Grade school	42%	22%	48%
High school	47	56	44
College	3	11	0
Other	3	0	4
No answer............	5	11	4

Table 22. Yes Responses of St. Martin Farm and Village Parents to the
Statements about Education of Children, 1951

Item	Yes Responses		
	Total	Village	Farm
(a) Grade school with reading, writing, and arithmetic is good enough for farming........	59%	34%	69%
(b) High schools take the boys and girls away from the farm..................	61	41	70
(c) Schools should offer more subjects of vocational interest to agriculture.............	79	78	79
(d) Children of today need more education.....	86	88	86
(e) The farm boy can learn all he needs to know about farming from his father.........	46	16	56
(f) Farming requires as much education as any other occupation.....................	63	66	63

ing from his father" (item e). Note also the high vote for "Children of today need more education" (item d). The responses are obviously in conflict, but it may be that the respondents read into the statements different meanings than were intended by those who designed them.

It was evident from the survey of St. Martin's parish that the villagers had somewhat higher educational aspirations than did the farmers. Indeed, the village family heads had somewhat higher education on the average than the farmers. With regard to farm work requirements, a modest test of the influence of this factor in this parish was obtained by using the number of milk cows as an index. Among those with the larger herds slightly more than a third favored high school compared with nearly three fifths of those with the smaller herds. The latter group perhaps had less possibility of keeping their children in farming and were willing to see them prepare for other careers.

The persistence of Old World values sometimes goes along with the continued use of the foreign tongue in the home. Families that used German at home were more inclined to view grade school education as sufficient than were those who used the English language.

A mainly Norwegian community: Rosewood. Rosewood is located in the northwestern part of the state near Thief River Falls. The inhabitants, seventy-one families, are mainly Norwegian. Although on the basis of the analysis of the counties already reported in this chapter, it appeared that the people of Scandinavian background might be more inclined to favor high school education, the results of the survey of Rosewood do not bear this out in all respects. For one thing, the children of the seventy-one families had not gone much beyond their parents in formal training. This was especially true of the boys, although the girls fared much better. Whereas over 75 per cent of the farm boys had had eighth grade or less education, and only 12 per cent had completed high school, only 35 per cent of the girls had eighth grade or less, while 42 per cent had completed high school.

In thirty-five of the seventy-one families the children had terminated their education, but the interviewer asked this question of the others: "How much education would you like your children to have?" Seventeen of twenty-five farm families with children going to school wanted them to have high school or better; five others would be satisfied with less than four years of high school, although they qualified their replies by many conditions such as "if the kid is smart," "if the boy is not needed on the farm," "if they want to go." Ten of eleven nonfarm families with children in school regarded high school education as the minimum. This is a more favorable attitude toward high school than that expressed by the parents of St. Martin's parish.

Asked about how much education is needed for farming, most of the 51 farm family heads were in favor of more than eighth grade, although 12 said one could farm without an education. Twice as many thought high school or agricultural school was needed — "Need all you can get," "Can't get too much." There was strong opinion against keeping the boy out of school to help on the farm: "Father should hire help if necessary."

Rosewood is located in an area of comparatively low productivity, and it could be that the families with children still going to school are looking to education as the best equipment to make a living either locally or away, more likely the latter. It is apparent that most of the farm youth will need to migrate to village or city to find employment.

A Finnish community: Wawina. This community in the northeastern part of the state is on land of low productivity. There were forty-two families in the sample, of whom sixteen were farming. Thirty-four of the family heads were of Finnish descent. The parental level of education was somewhat lower than in the other communities, particularly that of the men, one third of whom had sixth grade or less and none of whom had completed high school. This is in spite of the fact that the northeastern part of the state generally ranked high in attendance of 16–17-year-olds. Nevertheless, these parents were strongly in favor of education beyond the grades for their children. None was willing to say that eighth grade was sufficient for a boy and only one specified any conditions regarding high school, while twenty-nine said "high school unconditionally."

This overwhelming commitment to high school education for boys — and girls as well — was probably influenced by the knowledge that many if not all of the young people would need to find nonagricultural careers for themselves. There was a feeling expressed by some parents that little formal education was needed for farming and they tended to rate experience a trifle above education for success in that occupation. Many of the young people whose schooling has ended have left the community, which may suggest to the parents that education is after all a device by which young people may be assisted in finding more satisfactory adjustment in communities to which they may migrate.

A German Lutheran community: Moltke. Referring again to the analysis of data by counties, we recall the conclusion that ethnic-religious background appeared to be definitely related to attendance at high school, and that in some of the rich agricultural counties where people of German or Slavic descent were concentrated, the attendance tended to be low. Moltke was selected to represent a German Protestant group. It is on good land, located in Sibley County in the south-central part of the state. This community, contrary to expectations, revealed a relatively high level of education, especially of girls, one fourth of whom had had some college. However, over half of the girls had not gone beyond the eighth grade. As was true in the other places, both boys and girls had more education than their parents. But it is quite clear from the survey that nationality had not operated to produce an extraordinarily low level of education.

The conclusions from the four studies can be summarized as follows:

1. In the attendance of the 16- and 17-year-old boys and girls of farm parents St. Martin is low and the other communities are higher. The numbers are, however, too small to provide a conclusive test.

2. In regard to the favorability of farm parents toward education for farm boys beyond the eighth grade, St. Martin was lowest with 43 per cent, then came Moltke with 66 per cent, Rosewood with 69 per cent, and Wawina with 94 per cent.

3. There appears to be some relation between the occupation of farming and unfavorable attitudes toward education. The tendency to use the Old World language in the home — a reflection of the persistence of tradition — is also related to educational aspirations. It is highly probable, therefore, that as new generations come along the negative attitudes toward high school education will tend to disappear.

4. The data from the four communities are not uniformly in support of the idea that people of German and Slavic background are less favorable toward higher education than toward grade school education, but there is some indication that this is true.

A glance at the history of Minnesota leaves no doubt of the determination of the pioneers to provide elementary education for all children. In addition to performing all of the other tasks of building a new state, they succeeded in providing schools for practically all children by the close of the first half century. High schools and colleges were also established early, but the idea of making secondary education available for every child was not to become a reality until after the first hundred years. It is a problem for the future, but the trend forward is clearly indicated.

We have seen that in the decade from 1940 to 1950 the attendance at high school of farm boys and girls 16–17 years of age has markedly increased. This increase has been much greater than that among urban or village youth, so that the inequality is rapidly being overcome. The negative attitudes of parents toward post–grade school education that influenced low attendance are apparently giving way to the conviction that life in the modern world requires more education for farm as well as nonfarm children.

It has been a long march from the simple sod or log schoolhouse of the frontier to the modern structures housing the schoolrooms of mid-century Minnesota. Whatever differences of opinion now exist about the content of education, the fact must be noted that the schoolteacher of the 1950's is far better trained than the schoolmaster of the 1850's. The inadequate rural school district is rapidly giving way to the consolidated unit which makes more effective use of the tax funds and the facilities required by today's education.

Minnesota still has far to go in providing facilities and teachers for the next generation. Children born since 1945 are the most numerous in history, which means greater expenditure for school construction, teachers, and all the rest. The content of education for the critical period in which we live — which will probably continue to be critical for an indefinite future — is admittedly a problem of the first magnitude, but it is receiving the thoughtful cooperation of professionals and citizens alike, a condition necessary for solution. Minnesota's second century, no less than its first, demands continued dedication and effort if the oncoming generations are to represent progress rather than retrogression from the parental levels.

But communities consist of other institutions as well as schools. The most important institution in establishing and maintaining order is government, and the way in which its local units came into being is the subject of the chapter to follow.

VII Government for the People

INSTITUTIONS are made for man and not man for institutions. Government is a means to an end, and not an end in itself. Government of some kind is indispensable to society, not only as a device for control and regulation — a negative objective — but also, in recent times especially, as a device for collective action toward attaining numerous services. In this latter sense, it may be regarded as a means through which and by which people cooperate to satisfy many common needs. Farmers, for example, when they failed in their efforts to attain controls over their production by voluntary association, resorted to the use of government to achieve their ends. Education, highways, water and sewage systems, and many services are provided through government organization. There are numerous other ways in which government — local, state, and national — is being used to provide services at one time obtained individually or by voluntary association.

Certain attitudes toward government structure make adjustment and adaptation unusually difficult. Change is resisted in this institutional area as in no other. Even after the government's organization has become archaic and obsolete with the changing social order, and modifications are obviously needed, it is extremely difficult to introduce them. People are so conservative in this respect doubtless because of their latent fear that changes will bring into power persons who will annex privileges and immunities for themselves which most do not regard as right and just. Where changes in government structure seem to be needed, it becomes necessary, therefore, to make sure that any new rights and immunities given to officials by the changes will be appropriately safeguarded.

About thirty-five years ago Charles J. Galpin pointed out that "farmers have no effective municipality." [1] At the same time he might have said the farmer is a member of more governmental units than any other citizen. For example, in Minnesota he is typically a member of the following units: the school district, the town or township, the county, and probably a soil conservation district or some other special district. He is expected to vote for officers in all of these units, plus state and national officials. Yet it is true to say that he has no effective municipality.

The farmer's situation with reference to local government is, for the most part, the direct result of the pattern of settlement of the pioneer period. By pattern of settlement I mean the manner in which the land is occupied. The two fundamental patterns are the farm village and the scattered farmsteads. The farm village, fairly common in Europe and especially in Asia, is very uncommon in the United States. While the early New England settlers established themselves in villages, or towns as they were called, rather than on separate farms, this pattern did not prevail when people from these towns moved westward onto the new public domain. For the most part they established their homes on individual farms, farms that were most often 160 acres. Indeed the laws of the federal government under which title to land was conveyed to the settlers required that they establish residence on their claims. At least this was true for the Homestead Act of 1862 and the earlier Pre-emption Act of 1841.

The rectangular survey adopted by Congress in 1785, providing for the division of land into sections of 640 acres and townships of 36 sections, also influenced the evolution of local government. Although this method of dividing the land proved very effective in assuring each person a clear title to a specific tract without any overlap on any other claim, it made for a certain rigidity and inflexibility in arranging for social services. The families became scattered over a wide area. For example, in a township of 36 sections with four farms to the section, there could be only 144 families, and these scattered over a 36-square-mile area.

In the pioneer period, before all-weather roads and rapid transportation came into existence, it was necessary for people to establish their

[1] Charles Josiah Galpin, *Rural Social Problems* (New York: Century Company, 1924), p. 213.

schools, their churches, and their communities close to their habitations. It was inevitable, therefore, that the one-room school and the country church should come into existence. It was inevitable too that if the farmers were to have any kind of local government, the population would have to be small and dwell within an area small enough to make it possible — given the poor transportation facilities — for them to come together for consideration of their common problems.

The Minnesota County

The most universal form of local government in the United States is the county. Counties are self-governing units created by act of the state legislature. They also perform important services for the state government including the collection of taxes.

The first counties in Minnesota were created during the territorial period from 1849 to 1858. At the first session of the territorial legislative assembly in 1849 nine counties were established. Others came along in successive decades until the present total of eighty-seven was reached with the creation of Lake of the Woods County in 1922. It is a remarkable fact noted by William Anderson that sixty of the eighty-seven counties were established during the territorial period.[2] The year of full autonomous status of each county is shown in Table 23.

The rectangular survey with its gridiron pattern not only created the basis for what later became the organized towns but also for the counties themselves, because the towns or townships were the building blocks for the counties. Except where major physical barriers — rivers, lakes — intervene, the county boundaries followed the township lines. Although the counties vary greatly in size, the average in Minnesota amounts to around twenty-six townships.

Ideally a unit of local government should conform to some natural social or community area. Community area means the territory within which there is more social contact and interaction than there is among the people of this and other localities. Good examples of these natural social areas are the trade centers and the farm population that customarily comes to them to trade; that is, to buy and sell, to see the doctor, to attend movies and churches, and above all to send their children to high school. Indeed, the high school attendance area is perhaps the

[2] William Anderson, *An Outline of County Government in Minnesota* (Minneapolis: University of Minnesota Press, 1927), p. 2.

101

Table 23. Year of Attainment of Full Autonomous Status for the
87 Counties of Minnesota*

County	Date	County	Date	County	Date
Before 1860		Wright	1855	Watonwan	1871
Anoka	1857	*1860–1870*		Wilkin	1871
Benton	1851	Chippewa	1868	Yellow Medicine	1874
Blue Earth	1856	Douglas	1866	*1880–1890*	
Brown	1856	Mille Lacs	1863	Bigstone	1881
Carver	1856	Morrison	1867	Grant	1883
Chisago	1853	Pope	1868	Hubbard	1887
Dakota	1853	Redwood	1865	Kittson	1881
Dodge	1855	Renville	1868	Lincoln	1881
Faribault	1858	Sherburne	1862	Marshall	1881
Fillmore	1855	Todd	1867	Norman	1881
Freeborn	1857	*1870–1880*		Pipestone	1881
Goodhue	1854	Aitkin	1871	Stevens	1881
Hennepin	1852	Becker	1871	Traverse	1881
Houston	1854	Carlton	1870	Wadena	1881
Le Sueur	1856	Clay	1872	*1890–1900*	
Martin	1857	Cottonwood	1873	Beltrami	1894
McLeod	1856	Crow Wing	1871	Cass	1897
Meeker	1858	Isanti	1871	Itasca	1891
Mower	1856	Jackson	1870	Lake	1891
Nicollet	1855	Kandiyohi	1871	Red Lake	1896
Olmsted	1855	Kanebec	1871	Roseau	1894–1895
Ramsey	1851	Lac qui Parle	1878	*1900–1910*	
Rice	1858	Lyon	1875	Clearwater	1902
Scott	1855	Murray	1879	Cook	1901
Sibley	1855	Nobles	1873	Koochiching	1907
Stearns	1858	Otter Tail	1871	Mahnomen	1906–1907
Steele	1856	Pine	1872	*1910–1920*	
Wabasha	1855	Polk	1879	Pennington	1910
Waseca	1855	Rock	1874	*1920 on*	
Washington	1851	St. Louis	1873	Lake of the Woods	1922
Winona	1854	Swift	1875		

*The date of *original foundation* is sometimes a decade or so prior to the year
cited.

most important single criterion of the entity we call the rural community. Yet the ideal is seldom even approximated. Townships and even
county boundaries frequently cut directly through and divide a neighborhood or trade area community.

The organization of government. The organization chart of Goodhue
County (Figure 12) shows that county government is complicated. In
addition to the board of five commissioners who are elected for four
years, there are the following elective officers: coroner, register of deeds,
court commissioner, clerk of district court, and judge of probate court,

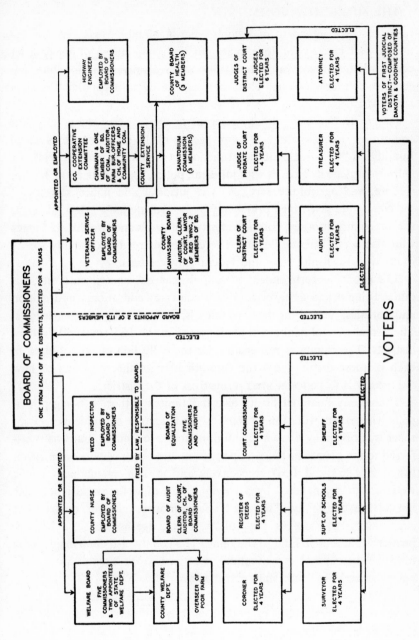

Figure 12. Organization Chart of Goodhue County, Showing Elective and Appointive Officials

103

surveyor, superintendent of schools, sheriff, auditor, treasurer, and attorney — all elected for four years. In addition, judges of the district court, where jurisdiction includes one other county with Goodhue, are each elected for six years. Then there are the various appointed officers and boards.

Functions. We have already referred to the fact that the county is a creature of the state and acts as an agency of the state in various ways. In addition "to its tax collection functions, Goodhue County provides or helps to provide its citizens with juridical, police, roads, education, health, welfare, and agriculture services. The juridical and police services of the county are performed principally by its probate judge, clerk of court, sheriff, county attorney, coroner, registrar of deeds and two district judges who also serve Dakota County. The county shares responsibility for its roads with township, state and federal governments." [3]

The county superintendent of schools has but limited authority, his duties being primarily associated with collecting educational information and statistics, supervising the rural schools, and enforcing attendance laws. The actual control of the schools is vested in the 155 (in 1940) school districts. The county is responsible for the collection of school taxes in each of these districts, but the determination of the rates and of how the money is to be spent are prerogatives of the district.

The county board of health also has limited authority, being principally concerned with the prevention and control of epidemics. Poor relief was originally a town function in Goodhue County, but was transferred to the county in 1858. A poor farm and an almshouse were established in 1863 and 1867 respectively and are still maintained. Public welfare is today handled by a county board of welfare and is a major financial responsibility. Two thirds of the money, however, comes from state and federal sources, particularly for old age assistance, aid to dependent children, and aid to the blind. The county also contributes some funds to the support of agricultural extension work but this work is financed mainly by state and federal funds.

Social organization. Mid-century Minnesota is characterized by a number of very diverse social organizations, both informal and formal. The situation in Goodhue County may be regarded as typical. Among the

[3] Frank D. Alexander and Lowry Nelson, *Rural Social Organization in Goodhue County*, University of Minnesota Agricultural Experiment Station Bulletin 401, 1949, p. 7.

formal organizations in this county, for example, were 83 churches representing 17 different denominations. More than half of these (44) were Lutheran, counting all synods. Ranking next in order were Roman Catholic 9, Methodist 7, Episcopal 6, and so on through the remainder of the denominations which have but 1 or 2 churches in the entire county.

There were 134 schools in operation in the school year 1946–1947, of which 123 were ungraded rural elementary institutions located in districts that maintained only 1 school each. Of these, 121 had but one teacher, 1 had two, and 1 had four. Of the 123 schools, 70 had fewer than fifteen pupils.

In addition to these formal institutions, there were 428 additional organizations representing a broad range of interests. Among these were 47 cooperative associations of all kinds, including purchasing, marketing, and service cooperatives. Some of these 428 organizations were limited in their membership to village or city people and others to farm population. A significantly large number, however, contained both town and country members. This joint membership was particularly common in large fraternal and benefit organizations, sports and hobby clubs, veterans' organizations, and welfare groups such as Boy Scouts and Girl Scouts.

The county as community. The extent to which a county operates as a community has been a problem for speculation among sociologists for a number of years. The interest arises particularly from the fact that counties, as pointed out earlier, are arbitrary instead of "natural" social units or areas. Nevertheless, the counties have become convenient units for the organization of some associations. Among these in Goodhue County, for example, were the County Health Association, the Goodhue County Historical Society, the County Horticultural Society, County Red Cross Chapter, County Veterans Service Committee, County Federation of Womens Clubs, County Democratic Farmer-Labor Committee, and the County Republican Committee. Primarily, however, these are town or village-centered organizations with relatively few farm families participating.

Even more village-centered are professional organizations such as the Goodhue County Medical Society and the County Medical Auxiliary, as well as the County Chapter of the Foundation for Infantile Paralysis and the County Beverage Dispensers Association. These organizations have no members among farm people at all.

The county is also the unit for the operation of various agencies of state and federal origin, such as those having to do with agricultural services. Among the latter are the Cooperative Extension Service, the Agricultural Commodity Stabilization Service, Soil Conservation Service, Farmers Home Administration, and the County Weed Inspector. (The last is a state official, whereas the former are either state and federal or exclusively federal agencies.) In addition there is the County Welfare Department which has a tie-up with the state and is supported in part by federal funds as well; the county health nurse, the Veterans Service Office, and the Minnesota Employment Service are organized on a county basis for convenience.

The county name serves as a symbol for identification for the inhabitants; as such it serves as a common bond among them. To the question "Where are you from?" the answer may be the name of the county. Most likely today the name of the village, town, or city will be given by dwellers in such places, but in earlier times the county name was more often used because the county was better known to people on the outside. Even today, however, a farmer, residing as he does in the open country, may feel as strongly identified with the county as with his nearest trade center.

Although there is this common identification of people with the county in which they reside, the more convenient basis for most organized social action is a smaller unit, especially the trade area community. This area, however, is not a governmental unit and will be discussed later.

The Town

As I mentioned earlier in this chapter, the unit of government nearest to the farm residents is the town. Its form is derived from the pattern established by the early settlers in New England. In New England, however, the towns were established as natural social areas, while in Minnesota and other states in this area, the town was laid out on the basis of the surveyor's township of 36 square miles, disregarding completely the social cohesion of the people. In Minnesota as in New England the town meeting is the governing authority. It has financial, legislative, and elective powers. Town meetings are held annually on the second Tuesday in March, when town taxes are voted and the amounts to be spent on roads and other services decided. The meeting may enact by-laws pertaining, for example, to the responsibility of property owners for animals running loose, and for some other local purposes of similar character.

One of its most important functions, of course, is to elect the several officers provided for the town by state law. These officials are a board of supervisors of three members elected for a three-year term, one to four overseers of highways, two justices of the peace, two constables, an assessor, a treasurer, and a clerk. All but the overseers of highways are elected for two years, the overseers for one. Some towns also have a pound master, health officer, weed inspector, town hall manager, deputy assessor, and deputy clerk. The compensation for town officers is on a per-diem basis or in the form of fees.

In 1930, according to William Anderson, there were 1,973 towns in Minnesota.[4] By 1940 the number had declined to 1,840, whereas by 1950 there were 1,844, and in 1957 or thereabouts, 1,828.[5] The trend in number over the years is obviously downward for two possible reasons: the decline in the farm population and the absorption of townships by incorporated places on the fringes of the cities.

It has been pointed out many times that the town is an inadequate unit of government to serve the needs of the population. Its tax base, as well as its population, is too limited to enable it to carry on the functions authorized by law. In the recent past the tendency has been for the functions of the town to be gradually taken over by the county, the state, or both. This is the case, for example, with welfare. Although there are still a few instances in which relief is administered by the town, in the vast majority of cases the county has become the unit for administering this function. Similarly, in the case of road and bridge construction and maintenance the county and the state have taken over more and more. The assessing of property, however, is still done by the town, although pressure is exerted from time to time to get the legislature to transfer this function to the county. Social control, policing, and the administration of justice are more and more taken over by the state highway patrol and the county sheriff's office. It is quite possible that in the not too distant future the county will become the only unit of local government except for the incorporated centers. Such a development is physically possible now, with rapid means of transportation and communication which the population did not have when the local units of government were established.

[4] William Anderson, *Local Government and Finance in Minnesota* (Minneapolis: University of Minnesota Press, 1935), p. 13.
[5] United States Bureau of the Census, "State and Local Government: Special Studies."

The Incorporated Village

Under the law in Minnesota, when a rural trade center has as many as one hundred inhabitants it may incorporate and receive a charter which grants certain authority to carry on the functions of local government. The low population limit makes this state one of the most incorporated in the nation. It is not too unlikely that dissatisfaction with the local town government is partly responsible for the drive to incorporate small places. When a village is incorporated, it becomes separated from the jurisdiction of the town government. In 1940 there were 201 places with fewer than 250 inhabitants, the average population of which was 169 people. They constituted 27 per cent of all incorporated places, and contained 1.9 per cent of the population. The number of incorporated places with fewer than 250 inhabitants increased from 201 in 1940 to 223 in 1950. In the latter year this group of villages made up 28.5 per cent of all incorporated places in the state, but contained only 1.7 per cent of the population.

Officers of villages are elected on the first Tuesday after the first Monday each December. The officers are three trustees elected for three-year terms, a clerk elected for two years, and a mayor for one year. These five constitute a village council. In addition, the following officers are elected: members of a board of education, assessor, treasurer, two constables, and two justices of the peace. The council may appoint an attorney, pound master, street commissioner, cemetery keeper, fire chief, marshall, policeman, and board of health. The names of the officers indicate some of the functions that the village government performs, such as the maintenance and repair of streets and bridges, keeping the peace, and meting out local justice. Some villages also maintain municipal light or gas plants. Villages also become school districts and education thus becomes another of their functions. Providing water and disposing of sewage, as well as general sanitation, likewise fall on the village council.

Here again, as in the towns, the number of people in the village is frequently so small and the tax base so limited as to make it difficult if not impossible to keep up these services at the level the population desires, and, by acceptable standards, ought to have.

The proportion of Minnesota's population which is not included in incorporated villages and cities has declined steadily since 1890. The total population living in unincorporated territory has increased, but not so rapidly as the population as a whole. It is an impressive fact that in 1950

Table 24. Number and Percentage of Minnesota's Population in Unincorporated Territory and in Incorporated Places Smaller Than 2,500 Persons, 1890–1950

Year	Total State Population	Unincorporated No.	%	Places of Less Than 2,500 No.	%	Percentage Rural Farm Is of Unincorporated Territory*
1890	1,310,283	714,887	54.6	152,347	11.6	...
1900	1,751,394	890,252	50.8	263,042	15.0	...
1910	2,075,708	899,248	43.3	326,166	15.7	...
1920	2,387,125	967,263	40.5	368,269	15.4	92.2
1930	2,563,953	965,990	37.7	340,347	13.3	91.9
1940	2,792,300	1,013,674	36.3	388,528	13.9	89.4
1950	2,982,483	964,763	32.3	410,274	13.8	76.7

*Rural farm population was not enumerated separately before 1920.

nearly a million Minnesotans were living in unincorporated territory (townships or towns are not considered incorporated areas). Naturally, this means that they were dependent upon town and county governments for local services. Over three fourths of this population belonged to the rural farm group. The percentage of the state's population in unincorporated territory has declined, however, from 54.6 per cent in 1890 to 32.3 per cent in 1950 (see Table 24).

The School District

School districts, like most other special districts, are created to perform a single function, in this case the establishment and maintenance of schools. For this purpose the district is authorized to elect trustees or boards, to levy taxes, to provide schoolhouses, and to employ teachers. We have already noticed that the scattered dwellings of the early settlers made it necessary to establish small institutions for the purposes of education, religion, and the like, in order that they might be within easy reach of the inhabitants (see also Chapter VI).

School districts were especially numerous in the early history of Minnesota, and were much smaller than the township — often within the 36 square miles there would be a half dozen or more. The number reached a peak in 1910, has been declining steadily since that time, and has fallen off at an accelerated rate since World War II (see Table 25).

Other Special Districts

Special districts in Minnesota in 1957 numbered 92, an increase from 71 in 1952; most of the increase was in soil conservation districts. Other special districts include housing, drainage, irrigation, water and sewer, and soil conservation. There may be still others which are not reported to the census.

As is true of school districts, authorization is granted by special act of the state legislature to form special districts and to elect officers, and otherwise to take action toward accomplishing the purpose for which

Table 25. Number of Government Units in Minnesota, 1890–1957

Year	Total Units	Counties	Towns	Incorporated Places	School Districts
1890	7,382	80	1,327	265	5,710
1900...........	8,812	82	1,529	451	6,750
1910...........	10,534	86	1,814	644	7,990
1920...........	10,610	86	1,852	692	7,980
1930...........	10,562	87	1,973	727	7,775
1940...........	10,359	87	1,840	745	7,687
1950...........	9,198	87	1,844	782	6,485
1952...........	9,236	87	1,883	787	6,479
1957...........	6,210	87	1,828	826	3,469

Source: William Anderson, *Local Government and Finance in Minnesota*, (Minneapolis: University of Minnesota Press, 1935, pp. 17–18); Bureau of the Census, "Governments in the United States," 1942, 1952, and 1957. The number of school districts for 1957 in this table does not correspond with that given the author by the State Department of Education, probably due to different dates of reporting.

they are created. Sometimes such authorization includes the sale of bonds on the security of the property within the district in order to obtain funds to accomplish the purpose, such as the drainage of swamp lands. Taxes are then levied on the district property to retire the bonds.

Trends in Local Government

The most conspicuous trend in local government is the decline of the number of units. Since 1940, for example, the number has declined by 4,218 (see Table 25). During the same period, the population of the state has increased by 700,000; thus there are more people per unit of government. In 1940 there were 360 and in 1957, 1,000 persons per unit on the average. The decline has important implications.

The loss of 4,218 units of government means a loss in several times that number of elected and appointed officials. It also means that responsibility for certain functions, notably education, has been shifted from a small group of citizens to a larger one. The presumption is that with a larger population and revenue base the function can be performed more efficiently. This trend is often referred to as centralization, and is opposed by many citizens on the ground that it removes the government farther from the people. The opponents of centralization assume that the more units of government you have, the more democracy exists. The proponents of centralization insist that the numerous small units of government are no longer adequate to perform the functions which the people are demanding. They have neither the population nor the revenue base to accomplish their purposes. Moreover, such small units, however justified they were in the pioneer period when poor transportation and communication were barriers, are no longer necessary. The proponents of more efficient units of government argue that there are probably twice as many counties in Minnesota as would be needed if rational planning could be substituted for political maneuvering, and that the more than 1,800 towns could and should be dispensed with entirely.

A Possible New Governmental Unit

Yet if the reduction in the counties and the elimination of the towns were to take place, some substitutes might be needed. Galpin has recommended that the trade areas be made the corporate entities. This would mean expanding the corporate boundaries of all the present trade centers — or some of them — to include the farm people living in the hinterland. What might with some convenience be done is to incorporate for all purposes the consolidated school districts. This would mean that the boundaries of the municipality would then be coextensive with those of the school district. There are obviously some questions which would need to be answered, such as the levying of taxes on farm and nonfarm property for the maintenance of certain services. Farmers would not be expected to pay for the village's water and sewage disposal. But they would want to pay for the maintenance of a fire department which could serve the entire area, farm and nonfarm alike.

Such a plan would bring village and farm people into close collaboration to support other services than education, and many opportunities for more and better services would result. It seems worth considering. Town and country are really not independent anymore, if they ever were. They are brought into closer relation with each passing year. Many members of farm families are employed in villages and towns; increasingly, town and country are joining in the support of schools and churches. The so-

111

cial and economic bases, it would appear, are being laid for the super-imposition of political or governmental institutions to conform with them.

But, although this suggestion is over forty years old, it has not been tried anywhere. More aggressive discussion of the idea is called for. Also, research is necessary and desirable to ascertain people's attitudes toward various local units — neighborhood, township, village, trade center. Such a study was attempted in Cannon Falls and its trade area, in Goodhue County. Roy C. Buck interviewed 225 families in the winter of 1948–1949 to discover the units of local social life with which they tended to identify themselves and something of the strength of that identification. He concluded that: (1) There was a significant relationship between lo-cality group identification and trade activity. While people showed strong loyalty to the neighborhood group, this was not to be regarded as incon-sistent with identification with the trade area or trade center. (2) Those who made the largest number of trips to the trade center during a week showed a somewhat higher degree of identification with the center: the activities of trade appear to bring farm people into closer identification with the center. (3) There appeared to be no relation between the strength of identification and distance from the trade center.[6] That is, those who lived farthest from the center identified themselves as strongly as those closer in.

Further studies would shed further light on citizens' attitudes toward this proposed new governmental unit. Many of the people in the trade area of Cannon Falls seemed to be favorable. No attempt was made during Buck's study to get the respondents' opinions about the specific proposal to incorporate the trade area.

The general opinion among students of local government in Minne-sota is that there are too many units of the wrong kind and not enough of the right kind. Town governments which may have been reasonably adequate in horse-and-buggy days are obsolete in mid-twentieth century. There are telling arguments against the proposition that they were ever adequate. Nevertheless, farm people have survived their inadequacies. Perhaps this is true only because the county and the state have taken over the performance of services for the localities which the towns were unable to handle. The towns show great powers of survival. It is probably

[6] For other conclusions and a complete report of the study see Roy C. Buck, "An Approach to the Measurement of Locality Group Identification in a Rural Trade Area," unpublished Ph.D. thesis, University of Minnesota, 1950.

only because of the overflow of cities onto their jurisdictions and their subsequent incorporation as villages that the number has declined as much as it has. They still persist in the rural farm areas, because there has been no suitable alternative offered.

Such an alternative has been suggested in this chapter. If serious thought and study are given to the proposition of creating municipalities out of the attendance areas of high schools, some tests should follow. One of the sources of vitality of political democracy is the possibility of experimentation with new forms of organization. In any case, there is much room for improvement in the present structure of rural government, and much need to search for better alternatives.

viii The Churches: From Cabin to Cathedral

R ELIGION, being a matter of the mind and spirit, is readily transported across the world. It is charged no freight by sea or land carriers; it is subjected to no customs duties at international frontiers. It was with the first settlers on Minnesota land, in their cabins on the prairies or in the forests. And by the subtle ways in which human beings transmit their culture through the generations, it is with the children of the pioneers a century later in their fine chapels and cathedrals.

Minnesota has drawn its various and numerous brands of organized religion from as many lands as its people have come from. Almost exclusively Christian, Minnesota's rural inhabitants professed in 1936[1] affiliation with no fewer than ninety-seven different groups. In this respect it was one of the most diversified populations in the nation.

Early History

Some priests and pastors preceded the plow, but in most cases they came after the plowmen were already there and established on their new farms. Among the earliest white visitors to Minnesota land were the Jesuit and Franciscan friars who came to convert the Indians. Father Louis Hennepin, a Franciscan monk from Belgium, came in 1680, plotted the river routes, and discovered the falls on the Mississippi to which he

[1] The date of the last official *Census of Religious Bodies*, taken by the United States Bureau of the Census. Congress authorized such a census to be taken every ten years, but after providing funds for those of 1906, 1916, 1926, and 1936, it failed to follow up with appropriations for 1946 or 1956. As a modest substitute for this failure of Congress, the National Council of Churches of Christ undertook a census of its own for 1956.

gave the name of St. Anthony. On his return to Belgium he wrote a best-selling book describing Minnesota. The first Christian mission was established in 1727 at Lake Pepin.

Almost a century later, Protestant missionaries came, devoting themselves first to bringing white civilization to the Indians in the form of education, sanitation, and clothing and food habits, and somewhat incidentally to converting them to Christianity. A Presbyterian clergyman, invited and encouraged by the American Fur Company, in 1832 established at Sandy Lake Minnesota's first school for Indian and half-breed children. In 1836 the same clergyman, Frederick Ayer, established a mission at Lake Pokegama in Pine County. Congregational missionaries in 1832–1834 established missions at Lake Itasca and Leech Lake. Methodist Episcopal missionaries worked among the Chippewa as early as 1839, and in 1850 Episcopal missionaries came to St. Paul and established several schools in the area, including Shattuck at Faribault.

One of the very important Roman Catholic missionaries of the early nineteenth century was Father Francis X. Pierz, who came in 1838, worked among the Indians, and is credited with being largely responsible for bringing the Benedictine monastery to what is now Collegeville. A large migration of Roman Catholics to the state followed upon the unification of Germany and the attempts by the new nation under Prussian domination to suppress the Roman Catholic Church. Stearns County became the center of a very important colony of Germans from Bavaria, Westphalia, and other Catholic states of the new Germany. They were accompanied or preceded by priests so that organized church activity was established from the beginning.

Lutherans and other Protestants came also in large numbers from Germany, but they were outnumbered by the more numerous Lutheran immigrants from the Scandinavian countries, especially Sweden and Norway. The first Swedish Lutheran churches were established in Center City, Chisago County (1854) and at Vasa and Red Wing in Goodhue County (1855). Although the first resident pastor served the Center City church beginning one year after it was established in 1854, the Lutheran flocks were mostly without shepherds in the early days. The state churches of the countries they came from showed little interest in them after they emigrated and the governments themselves even sought to discourage their departure from the homeland.

In the new settlements, therefore, they had to provide their own church

115

services under the leadership of selected laymen. Like so many other problems of pioneering, those of religious ritual had to be met as best they could with the resources at hand. Who was to administer the rite of baptism? Who was to serve at communion? Who was to marry couples? And what about the ministrations to the dying and the dead? With no authorized pastor of the church available there was only one thing to do: one of the brethren must perform these functions. The foundations of organized Lutheranism in Minnesota were laid in this manner by officiating laymen whose authority was recognized by the community. Later came ordained clergymen from abroad, but as rapidly as possible seminaries were established on American soil.

The other Protestant churches — Presbyterian, Congregational, Methodist, Episcopal — already had established sources in America for their ministers, so that their problem of supply, while serious, was not so acute as that of the Lutheran churches.

Religions Represented [2]

In few other states are the Roman Catholics, Lutherans, and other Protestant bodies so evenly matched in size as in Minnesota. While it is known as a center of Lutheran influence, Minnesota contains about as many Roman Catholics as Lutherans. In 1936 the reported church membership was 36 per cent Roman Catholic, 37.7 per cent Lutheran, and 26.3 per cent all others. The "all others" category included some Jewish and Eastern Orthodox congregations but for the most part it was composed of Protestants. The comparable percentages as reported in 1956 are Catholic, 38; Lutheran, 41; all other, 21. It would appear from these figures that the Catholics and Lutherans are gaining at the expense of the other groups, but statistics on religious affiliation being what they are, any such generalization would be lacking in caution. Statistics on church membership rely on voluntary reports from churches and cannot be regarded as complete. Churches differ in their definitions of membership. Some include all baptized persons as members and in some groups, such as the Roman Catholic, this means newborn infants. Other churches consider only those confirmed as members. Various age groups therefore are included or excluded according to the definition used. The Minne-

[2] Data are from the *Census of Religious Bodies*, 1936 and previous years; those for 1956 are from the census made by the National Council of the Churches of Christ.

sota Poll, which interviews only adults, reported the following percentages in their August, 1950, sample of one thousand persons, which was nearly double their usual sample:

Catholic 26.0%
Lutheran 35.5
Jewish 1.5
Other Protestant 34.0
Other and no church........... 3.0

The poll found a comparable distribution of the various groups in their regular sample of six hundred individuals in July and December, 1950. Among the Protestant churches other than Lutheran, the Methodists rank first, followed in order by the Presbyterians, Congregational Christian, Baptist, and Episcopalian; the five groups combined constitute about a sixth of all members. The Roman Catholics and the Lutherans, together with the five major other Protestant bodies, compose over ninety per cent of the church members of the state.

Sectarian Diversity

Although more than ninety per cent of the church membership is represented by the few major denominational groups, the remainder are divided among numerous sects. There has been no enumeration by sect since 1936, at which time there were ninety-seven in all, including those mentioned above. It is hardly to be expected that the number has declined in the past twenty years. Although there have been a number of mergers, it is more than likely that the mergers have been offset by the rise of new groups, particularly the Pentecostal or "holiness" sects. The various Lutheran synods, some sixteen in number, are all represented in Minnesota, and three of the major ones have their national headquarters in Minneapolis: the Evangelical Lutheran, the Augustana Lutheran, and the Luther Free Church. There have been some mergers, and rumors of mergers, among Lutheran bodies in recent years.

Geographic Distribution

Most of the ninety-seven denominations reported in 1936 had both rural and urban congregations. However, fourteen were exclusively rural and twenty-six were exclusively urban. Among those with only urban congregations were the various branches of the Eastern Orthodox faith, the Negro churches, and the Jewish congregations. Some of the Pentecostal groups were also represented only in the cities. Among the entirely rural groups were the Mennonite, Apostolic Christian, Church of God, Seventh-Day Baptists, and some subgroups of Lutherans.

The distribution of all reported church members in the 1956 census, using the categories "metropolitan," "intermediate," and "rural," is shown in Table 26.[3] The Jewish congregations are practically all metropolitan,

Table 26. Distribution of Church Members in Minnesota, 1956, and Total Population, 1950

Religious Body	Metropolitan	Intermediate	Rural
All faiths (1956).............	40.7%	46.4%	12.9%
Population (1950)............	44.3	43.3	12.4
Roman Catholic..............	47.2	44.0	8.8
Jewish	99.1	0.9	0.0
All Protestant...............	34.7	49.5	15.8
Protestant groups with over 500,000 members in the U.S.*			
American Baptist...........	81.9	18.1	0.0
Congregational Christian.....	48.0	43.5	8.5
Evangelical and Reformed....	24.6	55.7	19.6
Disciples of Christ..........	40.1	56.6	3.3
Evangelical–United Brethren..	22.3	59.0	18.7
American Lutheran........	28.1	56.3	15.6
Evangelical Lutheran........	18.4	59.7	21.9
Missouri Synod Lutheran.....	23.1	60.1	16.8
United Lutheran............	79.8	17.3	3.0
Methodist	45.8	44.5	9.7
Presbyterian	50.7	40.1	9.2
Protestant Episcopal.........	69.4	29.4	0.9

Source: *Churches and Church Membership in the United States*, Series E, No. 2, 1958, National Council of Churches of Christ in the USA.
* No reason is given for the failure of this analysis to report the Augustana Synod.

with Roman Catholics strong also in the metropolitan and the intermediate areas and somewhat under-represented in the rural. The Protestants, by contrast, are strong in the intermediate and rural areas and comparatively weak in the metropolitan. The distribution of specific Protestant denominations is also shown.

The denominations which had a larger percentage of their members who were rural than the percentage for the total membership for the

[3] These categories of counties are those defined by the United States Bureau of the Census in 1950. "Metropolitan" in Minnesota means St. Louis, Anoka, Dakota, Hennepin, and Ramsey Counties. "Rural" means those that contain no center of 2,500 or more population. "Intermediate" includes all others.

state (12.9), were the Evangelical and Reformed (19.6), Evangelical and United Brethren (19.7), American Lutheran (15.6), Evangelical Lutheran (21.9), and the Missouri Synod Lutheran (16.8). American Baptist had no rural members and the Protestant Episcopal very few.

The distribution of church membership by type of farming areas of the state for 1936 and 1956 as well as the percentage of change during the two decades is shown in Table 27. Area 1 is the southeast; area 3

Table 27. Percentages of Total Population Who Were Church Members by Type of Farming Area, 1936 and 1956, and the Percentage of Change

| Area | No. of Members | | Percentage of Total Population | | Gain or Loss 1936–1956 | |
	1936	1956	1936	1956	Members	Total Population
1	144,211	204,298	52.6%	58.6%	41.7%	27.3%
2	245,520	311,264	65.8	70.7	26.8	18.1
3	99,523	135,794	54.3	67.8	36.4	9.3
4	109,898	141,611	58.8	72.9	28.9	3.8
5	63,409	81,062	44.1	45.2	27.8	24.7
6	87,404	105,526	49.6	59.9	20.7	0.1
7	53,856	74,831	47.1	61.2	38.9	6.9
8	152,861	194,032	38.4	44.5	26.9	9.6
9	395,980	564,835	46.7	49.1	42.6	35.7
Total .	1,352,662	1,789,143	50.1	55.8	32.3	20.4

Source: *Churches and Church Membership in the United States*, Series C, No. 20, 1958, National Council of Churches of Christ in the USA.

is the southwest, and areas 2 and 4 are in between. These four areas make up roughly that part of the state south and west of the Twin Cities, including the first tier of counties north of Hennepin County. Area 9 is Hennepin and Ramsey Counties. The other areas — 5, 6, 7, and 8 — are the northern half of the state (see Figure 4). Outside of area 9, it will be seen that the greatest concentration of church members in relation to the total population is in the southern half of the state.

Membership is somewhat related to density of population: the greater the number of people per square mile, the higher the percentage reported as church members. There is some logic in this. Where the population is scattered, the difficulty of maintaining congregations and church attendance is obvious. In the northern part of the state where the number of persons per square mile is low, the percentage which belongs to churches is also low. See, for example, the figures for areas 5 and 8 especially.

Church Membership Grows Faster Than Population

One of the most interesting developments in the United States in recent years is that church membership has been increasing more rapidly than the population. This is also true of Minnesota. The *Census of Religious Bodies, 1936* reported as follows the percentages of the population who belonged to churches: 1916, 41.2; 1926, 48.4; 1936, 50.1. When we compare the census of the National Council of Churches for 1956 with the estimated Minnesota population for that year, we get a percentage of 55.8. This is a remarkable increase, but is still somewhat less than that estimated for the United States (62.0). However, the differences are at best relative owing to the inadequacy of the basic data. Table 27 shows that the percentage increase in members for each type of farming area was greater than that for the population of each area. In fact, in area 6, where the estimated population declined, there was a gain of 21 per cent in church members.

While total membership of churches has been climbing, the number of churches has decreased. This means that the membership of each church has grown. In 1906 there were 4,721 churches reported with an average membership of 191; in 1956 there were 4,343 churches with an average membership of 414. For Protestants the average membership was 308, ranging from an average of 91 in Aitkin County to 614 in Hennepin. For Roman Catholics the average membership for the state was 926, ranging from 153 in Cook County to 2,654 in Ramsey.

The average size of rural and urban congregations is available for 1926 and 1936, but not for 1956. The average for urban churches in 1926 was 488 and in 1936, 529; comparable figures for rural churches were 170 and 185, respectively. Clearly, the trend toward fewer and larger churches is apparent in rural as well as urban areas.

A special analysis of twenty Protestant denominations for the years 1941 and 1946 was made by the Rural Sociology Department of the University of Minnesota by urban, village, and open-country churches. The results are shown in Table 28.

There was a modest increase in churches in villages and cities during the war years which offset a considerable decline in open-country churches. Membership increased in all categories, as did the member-

120

ship per church. The long-term trend toward fewer and larger churches among Protestants is again evident and is favorable to the future success of congregations. While the abandonment of open-country churches has no doubt been accelerated since the data for 1946 were assembled, it is very likely that the average membership for the village and open-country churches has increased, along with that in the urban centers.

Reasons for the Growth in Membership

Much interest has been aroused among students and others by the year-by-year tendency for membership of churches to rise faster than the increase in total population. A new atmosphere of piety seems to have descended upon the country during and since World War II. Churches which had a struggle to finance their operations during the depression years find themselves well supported by ever-growing congregations and larger per capita contributions. New chapels have sprung up across the

Table 28. Total Adult and Confirmed Membership and Average Number of Members, 1941 and 1946 (20 Denominations)

Location of Church	No. Churches Reporting		Total Membership			Membership Average		
	1941	1946	1941	1946	Increase	1941	1946	Increase
Urban	936	958	332,132	363,828	9.5%	361.4	384.2	6.3%
Village	1,558	1,575	207,901	222,887	7.2	137.3	144.3	5.1
Open-country .	1,143	1,118	118,831	119,527	.6	106.9	108.7	1.7
Total	3,637	3,651	658,864	706,242	7.2	185.9	196.6	5.8

land. Parochial schools seem to be flourishing. Books on peace of mind and soul grace the best-seller lists. Congress by law incorporates the name of God in the pledge of allegiance to the flag, and cabinet meetings, we are told, are opened by prayer. Surely a revival seems to be in full swing. The Reverend L. B. Wilson of the National Presbyterian Church in Washington, D.C. speaks of "unprecedented religious activity" which to him implies a new dedication to "human and spiritual values never before reached."

Here and there some church leaders view this "unprecedented religious activity" with some caution as an indicator of deep spiritual renaissance. But nobody denies the increased activity. What its deeper meaning may be is another question. Without presuming to judge the validity of the revival

121

on these grounds, it is worth noting that certain demographic changes can account for much of the new activity (see Table 29).

First, it is necessary to ask ourselves who it is that constitutes the major support for the churches. According to such piecemeal data as are available, the following groups participate proportionately more in church life: women, citydwellers, the better-off economically, the better-educated. Women, it is well known, are increasing faster than men; strangely, there were fewer men 15 years of age and over in the Minnesota population in 1950 than in 1940, while the women of this group increased by nearly 50,000.

Table 29. Some Demographic Changes in Minnesota among Population Segments over 14 Years of Age, 1950 and 1940

| | No. of Members | | |
Group	1950	1940	Difference
Urban	1,219,345	1,095,167	124,198
Male	577,345	524,848	52,497
Female	642,000	570,319	71,681
Rural nonfarm	431,970	369,036	62,934
Male	215,030	187,501	27,529
Female	216,940	181,535	35,405
Rural farm	495,075	638,949	−143,871
Male	276,735	363,127	−86,392
Female	218,340	275,819	−57,479
State	2,146,390	2,103,149	43,241
Male	1,069,110	1,075,476	−6,366
Female	1,077,280	1,027,673	49,607
High school education or better			
Male	79,850	76,173	3,677
Female	106,490	101,501	4,989

Source: *U.S. Census of Population* for 1950 and 1940.

As we saw in the chapter on education, there has been a marked rise in the level of formal schooling. This is further demonstrated by the increase of 8,666 persons with high school education or more between 1940 and 1950. No doubt this figure has risen greatly since 1950, but no later data are available.

No statistics are required to convince anyone that there has been a general upgrading of income in the population. By 1950, a larger proportion of families were in the middle and upper income levels than in 1940. A national survey made in 1952 by a professional polling service for the *Catholic Digest* showed that 25 per cent of the upper income group did not attend church, compared with 31 per cent of the middle, and 38 per cent of the lower income group. Other surveys have shown similar results.

Perhaps the most important factor has been the growth of the urban and village (mostly rural nonfarm) population: an increase of 124,198 urbanites in Minnesota in the decade, plus 62,934 rural nonfarm (mostly village). The fact that dwellers in city and town are more frequent participants in church activities should not be interpreted as reflection upon the piety of the farm population. The more likely explanation is that the greater activity of the nonfarm population results from their having easier access to formal church institutions. Some observers have also remarked that there is prestige associated with church attendance which is more important in the highly competitive urban society than in the agricultural areas.

I have used the census data for indicating trends from 1940 to 1950. This has been unavoidable, although it would have been ideal if I could have had comparable data for 1936 and 1956, the years I have used in marking the growth of church membership. The annual growth in church membership during the twenty-year period was 22,274. The annual increase in women 15 years old and over during the decade was about 5,000, while that of high school graduates and above was about 860. Of course some of these latter were women, so this figure could not logically be added to the increase of women. The annual increase of the urban and rural nonfarm population 15 years and over was about 19,000.

Trends similar to those for Minnesota can be shown to exist nationally. As I said earlier, I do not pretend that these demographic changes account for all of the religious revival. No doubt the mid-century population strives unusually hard for answers to personal and social problems — answers which are not to be found in the research laboratories or in the conclusions of science. The problems are beyond science, beyond the power of man to reduce to formulas or logic. Such dangers as the nuclear weapons, national leaders devoid of the traditional moral scruples, the uncertainties of a world of limited resources where population increase threatens survival — all these and other considerations without doubt contribute to a "return to religion" as a solace for anxiety. Whether the future years will show either continued growth in formal religious activity or a reaction into inactivity born of disillusionment will be observed by students of this most interesting and very important social institution.

The great diversity of denominations in the United States, and in Minnesota as well, derives in large part from the predominance of Protestantism. The tradition of dissent has marked American culture from the first days of the settlement of the New World. Coupled with this tendency to "protest" and to form new churches, is another factor in sectarian diversity: the multiplicity of ethnic strains which have participated in the formation of the new society — for each ethnic group brought its own religious organization and sought to perpetuate it in the new land. Thus in Minnesota, among the Protestant faiths, there are numerous Lutheran groups which are associated with the countries of their origin, and also Baptists and Methodists of various national derivations.

But the mood of mid-century Minnesota in religion is cooperation and a tendency toward assimilation. This is manifest in the steady decline of the number of churches, in spite of rapid increases in membership. It is manifest also in the merging of the churches at all levels — local, regional, and national. The non-Lutheran Protestant groups cooperate at the state level in their field services to local churches, often sponsoring the cooperation of several churches of different denomination in a local area for such purposes as the employment of a supervisor of religious education or a director of activities for young people. This device of the "larger parish" would have been unthinkable in earlier days, when denominational competition for dominance in new settlement areas was at its height. State cooperation is encouraged and facilitated by joint efforts at the national level. Various Lutheran groups, while maintaining their denominational identity, cooperate in welfare and educational work, at both state and national levels.

Cooperation among or mergers of churches which derive from particular national backgrounds — notably the various Lutheran bodies — is becoming increasingly possible because of the advance of assimilation. Only a few years ago the Norwegian Synod changed its name to Evangelical Lutheran Church. The decline in the frequency of services conducted in the Old World languages is further evidence of assimilation. While this has been a painful transition for the older generation, it has become necessary in order to hold the interest of the young people. It is obvious that as the churches become uniformly English-language churches, a serious impediment to cooperation, language differences, is removed. Doctrinal differences remain, of course, but these are being

124

lessened and in some cases compromises have been worked out which do not embarrass the cooperating groups.

While some of the older denominations are moving toward comity in their relations with each other, the sectarian pot is kept boiling by the rise of new sects. Indeed, some of these are growing more rapidly than the older congregations. The presence of the new groups is regarded with something less than enthusiasm by the established denominations, but in a sense they recapitulate the story of Christianity itself. At first despised by the established order, they achieve in time a measure of respectability and acceptance. Some of the new groups will disappear in time, others will coalesce to form even stronger associations. These in turn will view with jaundiced eye the rise of new sects, but ultimately they will recognize them. Thus the cycle of despised sect to respectable denomination goes on.

It should be registered as a mark of the growing maturity of American society that the persecution of new movements is less vicious and destructive than it was, say, two generations ago. A spirit of toleration — even of *tolerance* — is much more in evidence. It is much more generally recognized that in a democratic society the right to differ in matters of religion is as important as any other right specified in the Bill of Rights. Although there are still many who would like to deny the right of some of the newer sects to practice their religion, such persons are in the minority, and the minority seems to be declining.

Minnesota churches continue to provide, as they have always done, more social contacts for rural as well as urban people than any other single institution. Many persons who take little part in secular affairs do not neglect their relations with the church. In general, however, those who are most active in organized religious activity are also high participators in nonchurch affairs. The church, it is clear, is not only an organic part of the social structure, it is always an important, and often the most important, institution of the local community.

IX The Cutover: Our Rural Problem Area

No SECTION of the state of Minnesota is more attractive from the standpoint of scenic beauty and the opportunities it affords for all kinds of outdoor recreation than that which has long been referred to as the Cutover. (The favored designation now is the Northern Forested Area.) Moreover, no part of the state has a history which is garlanded with more romance or enlivened by greater adventure. It is truly a fabulous land of forests, of lakes and streams, of game and fish and wild fowl. It is a land where tens of thousands of people come each summer from far and near to enjoy exhilarating vacations. It is the source of a large part of the iron ore which feeds the steel mills farther east — ore of extraordinary richness which is transported through the Great Lakes during the summer months on giant oreboats. This part of the state contains the city of Duluth, with its magnificent harbor which serves the oreboats and boasts an annual tonnage which places it among the leading harbors of the nation. Its importance has been greatly enhanced by the opening of the St. Lawrence Seaway in 1959. The area is one of the main sources of timber for building and for manufacturing paper and other wood products. This resource also provides part- or full-time nonfarm employment. More will be said of this industry later.

But besides the resort services, the industrial complex associated with the mining, shipping, and processing of iron ore, and the timber resources, the Cutover is also important agriculturally. Farming is the sole occupation of many of its people; many others run farms and work part or full time in the mines, forests, and industries. It is notable for its high proportion of part-time farmers. Yet it is designated on the maps of the

126

United States as one of the areas of low farm income. It is a "problem" area because of the effort and capital required to clear the land of second-growth trees and shrubs; because of the climate, which is too cold for the economically competitive production of such crops as corn and soybeans; and because of the wide variation in soil types, often on the same farm. For these and other reasons, the area does not measure up to other sections of the state in agricultural productivity.

We have noted earlier that migration from the area is heavy in good times and light in bad. In short, the area is very vulnerable to the vicissitudes of cyclical fluctuations in the general economy. As long as jobs can be had outside, migration is large; but when there is a slowdown in nonfarm jobs, the migrants are dammed up in the home territory.

The settling of the Cutover is tied to the discovery and exploitation of two valuable and extensive resources: timber and iron. During the last half of the nineteenth century the axe and the saw all but completely devastated the virgin forests of the state. The annual cut of lumber increased gradually from 1850 to 1880, slowed only temporarily by the panic of 1857. After 1880 the volume rose abruptly each year until the turn of the century. "By 1889," says Stewart H. Holbrook, "lumberjacks numbered 112,000 in the 200,000 square miles of timberland" in the Lake States.[1] The increase in production in Minnesota after 1880 was largely the result of the lumber industry's moving into the northern part of the state, made possible by the completion of railroads to that area. Increased efficiency and technological improvements also made for increased production: the band saw was introduced, the logging cart with large wheels made summer logging possible, and other innovations came into use. Production reached its peak about the turn of the century, when an estimated forty thousand men "went into the timber."[2] After 1900 the annual cut declined abruptly. For one thing, under the Morris Act of 1902, 200,000 acres of forest were set aside as forest reserve (later the Chippewa National Forest) and a few years later 500,000 acres in Cook and Lake Counties were reserved, an area that became part of the Superior National Forest in 1909, after the national forest system was established.

In 1884, just as lumbering was rising abruptly in importance in the northeast, iron mining began in the Vermilion district. After the Mesabi

[1] Stewart H. Holbrook, *Tall Timber* (New York: Macmillan, 1941), p. 48.
[2] *Minnesota: A State Guide*, American Guide Series (New York: Viking Press, 1938), p. 92. This is for Minnesota only, not for the Lake States.

Table 30. Distribution by Country of Origin of 1920 Foreign-Born Population

Country	No.	Country	No.	Country	No.
Finland	17,344	Czechoslovakia	710	Netherlands	72
Sweden	12,339	Denmark	626	Poland	2,863
Yugoslavia	8,563	England	1,826	Rumania	92
Norway	7,188	Germany	1,928	Russia	2,178
Canada	6,812	Greece	601	Scotland	618
Italy	3,909	Hungary	280	Switzerland	98
Austria	1,368	Ireland	814	All others	1,186

deposits were discovered and operations had begun around 1892, the volume increased dramatically. The mining as well as the lumber industry created a great demand for labor. What occurred is illustrated by the censuses of St. Louis County, where so much of the activity took place. In 1880 in the entire county there were only 4,504 people. In 1890, there were 44,862; in 1900, 82,932; and in 1910, 163,274. Another 40,000 were added by 1920 when the population of the county rose to 206,391. Of the total population in 1920, 71,313 were from foreign lands, distributed as shown in Table 30. There were more than twenty countries contributing. The melting pot of the northeast was composed of many elements, all attracted by the chance for employment in the mines or forests or the possibility of acquiring land.

For in addition to the timber and iron, there was the land itself. Although its development was delayed by the dominant emphasis on lumber and ore, some farm settlement took place during the 1870's, since 378 farms were reported in the fourteen northeastern counties (including Pine) in 1880. Then began a rapid rise to 1,829 in 1890; 7,550 in 1900; 14,275 in 1910; 22,380 in 1920; 29,446 in 1925; and 25,994 in 1930.[3] The decline from 1925 to 1930 reflects industrial prosperity and the availability of nonfarm jobs. Obviously, many gave up farming in the Cutover, but the downward trend was cut short by the onset of the depression of the 1930's. By 1935, the number of farms rose to 34,040 and had declined but little by 1940 (33,601). Then came the war, which drew off farm people to army and factory, and the number of farms declined to 29,601 by 1945; to 24,579 in 1950; and to 19,736 in 1954. In the thirty-five years since 1920, the number rose from 22,000 to the high point of 34,000 in 1935 and then fell back below the count of 1920.

[3] Oscar B. Jesness, Reynolds I. Nowell, and associates, *A Program for Land Use in Northern Minnesota* (Minneapolis: University of Minnesota Press, 1935), p. 30.

THE CUTOVER: OUR RURAL PROBLEM AREA

Farming as a full-time employment is giving way before the attraction of nonfarm jobs outside and inside the area.

As lumbering declined, agriculture expanded and provided a refuge for those who remained when the center of lumbering moved to the far northwest. Yet agriculture has been less successful there on the whole than it has been in the areas more favored by soil and climate. The problem of clearing the land of the stumps and underbrush left in the wake of the loggers' devastation, and cutting the trees not considered of any worth by the timber men, was a costly undertaking for the settler. The percentage of "improved land in farms" reported by the census in 1900 was 19.4; by 1930, 30.0.[4] By 1945 what the census now calls "total cropland" was 35 per cent of all land in farms and by 1954, 37 per cent.[5]

These figures, together with those of many special studies, testify to the rugged task the farm operator faces in clearing his land. After sixty years, the cropland, which largely means cleared land, is still less than two fifths of the land in farms. Soils vary widely within small tracts. Much of the land is muskeg and swamp. Other parts are too sandy for high production, or contain too many rocks and boulders or basic outcropping to be useful for farming. Nevertheless, there are many thousands of acres of good soil interspersed with the poor, and on these lands many successful farms have been established. On the other hand, many unsuccessful farms have been attempted on the poor lands and later abandoned. The area has always been one of high mobility. People come in, get some land, try to farm it, and in the end some are forced to leave. Others come, make a success of farming, and remain. The results of studies made in 1956 will enable us to describe more fully the characteristics of the people, their problems, and their hopes and aspirations.

Rural Development and Interest in the Cutover

Many studies have been made of the agricultural problems and prospects of the area, and from time to time special programs have been undertaken with the idea that they would lead to the solution of problems. Special attention was given to the region during the 1930's when the depression and the drought brought chronic maladjustments to a

---

[4] *Loc. cit.*
[5] *United States Census of Agriculture* for 1945 and 1954. "Total cropland" includes cropland harvested, cropland not harvested and not pastured, and cropland used only for pasture.

critical stage. The latest concern has been expressed on a national scale in the Rural Development Program of the United States Department of Agriculture. Designed to assist farm people in low-income areas to make a more satisfactory adjustment to their resources, the program necessarily includes the Cutover.[6]

To facilitate planning for better use of the region's resources, the Department of Rural Sociology of the University of Minnesota undertook three related studies in 1956. One interviewed 575 farm operators, part-time and full-time. A second got information about the hopes and plans of the seniors in twenty high schools, sixteen in the Cutover and four in southwestern Minnesota. The latter came from what are probably the most productive agricultural counties of the state. A third study, using high school graduates from six high schools for 1948, 1950, 1952, 1954, and 1956, was an attempt to find out what the patterns of migration and the occupational experiences of the graduates had been over this period.

It is not my purpose here to do more than provide summaries and the conclusions of these studies. Details will be found in published articles and in those yet to be published. The emphasis of the investigations was on aspirations. What do the adults want for themselves and for their children? What does youth want to do in life? What impediments do they foresee to the realization of their ambitions? What outside assistance might be necessary? What does the fact that part-time farming is prominent in an area mean for the people concerned? What are the differences, if any, between full- and part-time farmers, socially and economically? These and many other questions were raised. In recent years there has been much discussion of ways and means of getting more people out of agriculture as a surplus-reducing measure. Some have suggested a government subsidy to get people to move off their farms. Such discussions are at "high levels" and usually not sufficiently concerned with what the people themselves think and want.

The Farmers of the Cutover

In order to facilitate the analysis of the data obtained from the 575 farmers, the thirteen northeastern counties were divided into two areas as shown in Figure 13. Area 1 consists of the counties in the eastern

[6] *Development of Agriculture's Human Resources: A Report on Problems of Low Income Farmers* (United States Government Printing Office, April, 1955).

section which were most strongly influenced by mining and timber operations and by the Duluth-Superior industrial and transportation complex; agriculture was less important relative to nonagricultural pursuits. Area 2 consists of the western counties where agriculture is relatively more important but where some influence of mining and industry is nevertheless felt. This section is also important for the tourist trade it attracts. Resorts

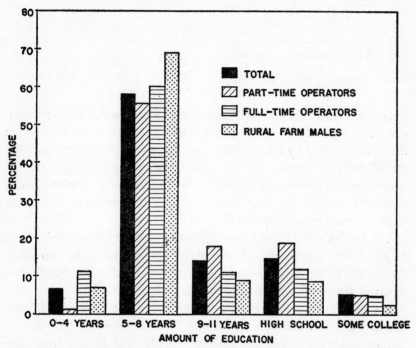

Figure 13. Number of Years of School Completed by Part-Time and Full-Time Farm Operators in Northeastern Minnesota Compared with the Average Education of Rural Farm Males, 1950

are important in the entire area, but more important in the western counties. (Area 3 is the Corn Belt of the state and was used as a comparative sample area for the study of high school graduates.)

Economic status. Because of its low average productivity, farmland in the Cutover tends to be cheap, and for the same reason the area has a high percentage of owner-operated farms. Full owners made up 70 per cent of the 1956 sample. Those who own some land and rent some (part-owners) made up another 26 per cent, leaving only 4 per cent

131

renters. There were only minor differences between the two areas, mainly due to more part-owners and more renters in area 2.

The operators had farms with a median 143 acres, with considerable variation by area and by part- or full-time (see Table 31). For the total

Table 31. Comparison of Median Acres and Median Cropland per Farm of Part-Time and Full-Time Operators, Area 1 and Area 2

	Area 1		Area 2	
	Part-Time	Full-Time	Part-Time	Full-Time
Median acreage.......	95	126	128	170
Cropland acreage......	43	54	38	85
Cropland	45.3%	42.9%	29.7%	50.0%

sample in area 1, the cropland made up 42.5 per cent of land in farms, compared with 45 per cent in area 2. These percentages are higher than the 37.2 reported by the United States Census of Agriculture in 1954 for all thirteen counties, but there are nearly three years between the census and the survey. The increase in the percentage of cropland can be credited largely to the disappearance during the period of farms with small percentages of cropland.[7]

The median value of land and buildings reported by these families was $6,879,[8] with a difference of only about $500 between the two areas. Again, this figure includes both full- and part-time farmers. Nearly two thirds of the farms were free of mortgage debt.

The median gross farm income for the total group was about $2,500, and no difference was reported between the areas: for part-time farmers income was $1,400, and for full-time, $3,440. The income from non-farm sources was markedly different: $3,480 for area 1 and $1,909 for area 2; $3,569 for part-time and $449 for full-time farmers. When all sources and amounts of family income are combined, area 1 again shows to advantage with $3,659 compared with $2,629 for area 2, a difference

[7] From 1950 to 1954 the acreage in farms in the thirteen counties declined by 9.7 per cent, while cropland declined by only 6.7 per cent, indicating that the 20 per cent decline in the number of farms represented farms with a low percentage of cropland. Also, farm operators who left may have sold or rented their cropland to those who remained, thus bringing up the total percentage of cropland for the whole.

[8] This figure compares with the average value of land and buildings per farm of $6,704 for this economic area as reported in the *United States Census of Agriculture*, 1954. The average for the state was $21,051.

of over a thousand dollars. The difference between the two types of operators is striking. It is impossible to get a statewide figure of gross farm income comparable to this. The nearest approach is that given in the census called "value of farm products sold." This total figure divided by the number of farms in the state was about $5,400. Again, the two figures are nearly three years different in time, and that for the state is an average while that for the survey is a median. The total family income of part-timers was $4,240 contrasted with $1,989 for full-time. For all combined it was $3,010. It is obviously the part-time employment in area 1 which brings the median up above the income of area 2.

This superior income of area 1 is reflected in the level of living, as measured by the Sewell Socio-Economic Status Scale (see p. 71). Of the homes in area 1, 53.4 per cent rate "high" and 18.5 "low," while the figures for area 2 were 22.8 per cent high and 38.2 per cent low.

These operators were asked to estimate their net worth — that is, what they estimated they would have left, after debts were paid, if they were to sell out. Estimates ranged widely from less than $1,000 to more than $30,000. There was no significant difference between the areas, but there was between the part-time and full-time operators. The median estimated net worth for both groups was $7,649 — for part-timers $6,800, for full-timers $8,299.

Residential mobility. Though, as I pointed out earlier, the counties of northeastern Minnesota are subject to greater fluctuations in population than other parts of the state, it is interesting to find that the farm operators surveyed are a very stable group. Two thirds of them were born in Minnesota; moreover, 36 per cent of the part-time and 32 per cent of the full-time farmers were born in the northeastern area; and 16 per cent were brought into the area when they were young — so that for all practical purposes it can be said that over half of all the operators are "native" to the area. The operators' median length of time in the county of residence was 32 years. There was little difference, if any, in the length of residence of part-time and full-time farmers that could not be explained by the younger average age of the former.

We shall probably never know how many people have come in, remained for short or long periods, and then moved out again. We have information only on those who were there in 1956; and they proved to be a very stable group indeed.

Why did you come to the Cutover? The operators who were not born

133

in the area or were not brought in as children ascribed their coming to several motives. The most important of these was cheap land. Vast acreages became tax-delinquent during the late 1920's and early 1930's, mainly as a consequence of the depression, and it was possible to acquire this land by paying the usually small taxes due per acre. Twenty per cent of all those interviewed gave cheap land as a reason for coming. A few (4.2 per cent) said the depression was a factor in their migration. We have referred to this influence in Chapter II, and to the build-up of population in the northeast. The importance of the back-to-the-land migration has never been considered very great. The increase in population which was observed during the depression years in this region is due more largely to the reduction in "normal" migration resulting from the lack of nonfarm job opportunities. Yet if we combine the two reasons for coming, cheap land and depression, they would account for a fourth of all reasons for being there, including being born there or coming as children. It would mean that half of those born elsewhere were attracted by cheap land and circumstances attendant upon the depression. Others said that they had relatives in the area or offered an assortment of more personal reasons for migration.

Farm background and work experience. Nearly four fifths of the operators were born on farms. In the vast majority of cases, either the operator's father, or his wife's father, or both, were also farmers. Only 9 per cent of the operators were children of parents neither of whom were of farm background. There was no difference between the two areas in this matter when part- and full-time farmers were combined, but there were considerable differences between the two operator groups when they were considered separately. The part-time operators reported that both their parents were farm-reared in 57 per cent of the cases compared with 65 per cent for the full-time. On the other hand, 11 per cent of the part-time and 8 per cent of the full-time operators said that both their parents were of nonfarm background. Whatever may have been the background of those who have come into the region and left again, certainly those who have remained have a strong tradition of farming: they are not refugees from the city.

Despite the fact that so large a proportion of the operators were sons of farmers — or of mothers who were daughters of farmers — most of them have come into farming after or during nonfarm work. In the total sample, only 29 per cent have been full-time farmers all or most of their lives, while another 6 per cent have always had a full-time nonfarm job while engaging in part-time farming. The remainder have gone from (a) farming originally to a nonfarm job for at least two years, then to part-time farming (8.3 per cent); (b) from farming to nonfarm job to full-time farming (5.0 per cent); (c) from full-time to part-time (7.7 per cent); (d) from nonfarm job to full-time farming (17.8 per cent); and (e) from nonfarm job to part-time farming (23.5 per cent).

It is interesting and instructive to note the great extent to which nonfarm jobs have prepared the way for the operators to enter farming. Well over half of the operators have apparently entered farming in this way, either part- or full-time.

Education. Over a third of the operators have had nine years or more of school. Three fifths have had from five to eight years of schooling, and it is fair to assume that all but a few of these are graduates of the elementary school. There are some interesting differences between the two classes of operators. Over ten per cent of the full-time operators completed less than four grades, compared with half of one per cent for part-time. Although there is but a small difference in the proportions of the two groups in the upper grades, the part-timers have 42 per cent with nine grades or more compared with only 29 per cent of the full-time men. Nearly 19 per cent of the part-time farmers, compared with 12 per cent full-time, were high school graduates; but about the same percentage in each category had had some college or postgraduate work or had other training such as attending a trade or business school. The difference in favor of the part-time operators was largely due to the fact that they were younger than the full-time operators. The group is generally better educated than were males over 25 in the Minnesota rural farm population of 1950. However, the level of schooling among farm people is rising rapidly and it is to be expected that the six years since the census was taken would result in some improvement (Fig. 13).

Social participation. The Farmers' Union has more members than the Farm Bureau in both areas, but the latter makes a better showing in area 2 than in area 1. It is important to note the high proportion of the group who belong to labor unions, symbolic of the disappearance of the occupational provincialism which characterized farm and nonfarm in the past.

When the part- and full-time farmers are tabulated separately, we discover some interesting differences. The part-time farmers are the high participants in unions, 43.5 per cent of them reporting union affiliation, compared with 2.1 for the full-time. On the other hand, 20.4 per cent of the full-time compared with 10.5 per cent of the others are active in farm organizations. But 60 per cent of the full-timers said they belonged to no organization, compared with 29 per cent of the part-timers. Here again, the comparative youth of the part-timers is doubtless a factor in their higher participation in organizations.

Visiting patterns differ by area as well as by our two categories of operators. Visiting is more with other farmers than with nonfarmers in area 2 compared with area 1, and slightly more of the area 1 operators reported no visiting. About a third of the part-timers visited with farmers exclusively, compared with almost half of the full-timers. On the other hand, nearly a fifth of the part-time operators reported visiting only with nonfarmers, compared with around a tenth of the full-timers. These differences in neighboring patterns should be significant to extension workers seeking to reach the part-time as well as the full-time operators.

Problems Listed by Farmers

Economists and others who have studied the area have been responsible for calling northeastern Minnesota a problem area. They arrive at their conclusions through the use of census reports and through special studies of their own or those made by others. They enumerate the problems and estimate their relative importance without consultation with the farmers. The survey made by the Rural Sociology Department in 1956 sought the judgment of the farmers themselves on this question by asking: What are the main problems the farmers in this area are faced with? The problems and the percentages who named them are shown in Table 32. Many farmers gave more than one reason. The large percentage whose problems come under "others" had various individual problems. Some of these were related to the other categories: "too many rocks on the land," for example, could be classed as low soil fertility in a broader sense. There are some differences between the two kinds of operators, but in general they are not great.

What to do about problems. When asked what should be done, farmers tended to focus on prices and credit. "Raise farm prices" got the largest vote, 30 per cent, and "better credit facilities" got 15 per cent. Over 7 per cent answered "nothing." "Adopt better methods" got 14 per cent, and improved public works, road building, and drainage got

Table 32. Responses of Full-Time and Part-Time Farmers of Northeastern Minnesota to the Question: What Are the Main Problems Farmers in This Area Are Faced with?

Problem	All Operators	Part-Time	Full-Time
Lack of capital............	52.0%	49.3%	53.8%
Too small farms...........	37.8	40.6	36.0
Short growing season......	28.6	33.3	25.5
Low soil fertility..........	27.1	25.1	28.2
Lack of market............	22.6	21.7	28.2
Lack of nonfarm work.....	3.3	0.5	5.1
Various others............	59.1	54.1	62.4

10 per cent. Clearing land was an important solution for another 10 per cent.

Who should do these things? "Farmers themselves," said 34 per cent, but a hefty 58 per cent said "the federal government." Only 15 per cent thought the state government should do the job. Naturally, it was too much to expect that with the complexity of the problems the farmers reported there could be a single answer. Farmers themselves *can* do some things, such as applying better methods in their work. Services are also available within the state which can be utilized to advantage. But prices and credit, which loomed so large in their thinking, are inevitably associated with the federal government.

What do you plan to do? Farmers were asked about their desire to remain in or move out of the area. (The question is significant for the Rural Development Program for the reason stated earlier, that much thought is centered on the prospect of promoting migration out of all problem areas.) Most of the northeastern farmers want to stay in the area — 85 per cent of them, in fact. The others would move, if they could get a good price for their farms, if they could get a good nonfarm job, if they could get better land, if farm conditions don't improve. It is quite apparent from the returns that there is no great dissatisfaction with the area among these people; at least, it is not intense enough to cause unrest. They seem to like it there.

However, when they were asked if they planned to stay in farming, only 55 per cent in area 1 gave an affirmative answer and 64 per cent in area 2. About 8 per cent were undecided. Thus, in spite of the strong vote for staying in the region, a large proportion would move out of agriculture as an occupation. Since opportunities for nonfarm jobs are better in area 1, apparently more would forsake the farm there than in area 2.

Only a small percentage intend to move away. The potential movers wanted to go west — to Oregon, Washington, Idaho, or California. In short, if they leave the area at all, they will leave Minnesota.

The relatively heavy vote for leaving farming for other work coincides with the expressed opinions about the future of agriculture: about ten per cent thought the outlook was favorable, about sixty per cent that it was generally unfavorable. The remaining thirty per cent considered the future would be "fair" or "about the same" for farming.

Conclusions about Farmers in the Cutover

There has been a continuous and marked decline in the number of farms. Though this decline is general over the state and nation, it has been more pronounced in the northeastern and other northern areas of Minnesota.

The decline in farms has been proportionately much greater than the decline in farm acreage or the decline in cropland. Thus the average size of farm has increased, as has also the average cropland per farm.

Part-time farming in the eastern portion of the area has increased and is made possible by the employment in mining, forestry, transportation, and industries based upon iron and wood.

The farm operators have a relatively long history of residence in the area, and all but a small proportion plan to remain there, even though a fourth to a third expect to withdraw from farming.

Over half of the farmers gave lack of sufficient capital as an area-wide problem, followed by the small size of farms, low soil fertility, lack of markets, and short growing season. Of the problems about which something might be done, such as credit and improved markets, the farmers were of the opinion that the federal government should take the responsibility, although some believed that the state government could do more, and a portion thought that farmers themselves should take the initiative.

The median incomes, value of land and buildings, and net worth of these farmers would undoubtedly fall below the averages for the state, if comparable figures were available for 1956. Nevertheless, income from nonfarm sources which supplements farm income brings median family income for the part-time farmers up to a level that does not spell hardship, although we must keep in mind the fact that there were as many families below $4,240 as above. The income of full-time farmers, a median less than $2,000, leaves something to be desired. The net worth is low, even though not more than a third of the operators reported any debt. The farms are not only smaller than the average for the state, but the value per acre is little more than a third of the state average, according to the census of 1954.

The farm operators appear to have better average education as of 1956 compared with the male population over 25 in 1950. This is partly accounted for by the time difference of six years, but may also be due in part to the generally high level of education in this area.[9]

The Young People of the Cutover

It is reasonably clear that farm operators want to stay in the Cutover. But what the young people want and what they will do will have much influence in determining the future. The 1,770 seniors in the sixteen high schools of the northeast and in four in the southwest (see Fig. 14) in the spring of 1956, answered some questions as to their own aspirations. They were also asked to give the occupation of their fathers. The responses by area are shown in Table 33. The deviation of the seniors

Table 33. Comparison of Vocational Aspirations of 1,770 High School Seniors and Their Fathers' Occupations *

	Area 1		Area 2		Area 3	
Occupation	Senior's Aspiration	Father's Occupation	Senior's Aspiration	Father's Occupation	Senior's Aspiration	Father's Occupation
Professional	43%	6%	38%	4%	36%	4%
Farming	1	7	2	23	10	34
Clerical	22	11	24	7	23	8
Proprietor	6	2	5	12	4	15
Skilled worker.....	6	25	8	19	8	18
Semi-skilled	7	14	7	18	7	8
Unskilled	1	8	1	9	1	4

* Only the major choices and occupations of fathers are given to indicate the trend. The complete data are on file in the Rural Sociology Office, Agricultural Experiment Station, University of Minnesota.

[9] See Chapter VI, and Lowry Nelson, "Education of the Farm Population in Minnesota," Minnesota Agricultural Experiment Station Bulletin No. 377, 1944; Douglas G. Marshall and Milo J. Peterson, "Are Minnesota's Farm Youth in School?" Minnesota Agricultural Experiment Station Miscellaneous Journal Series No. 582.

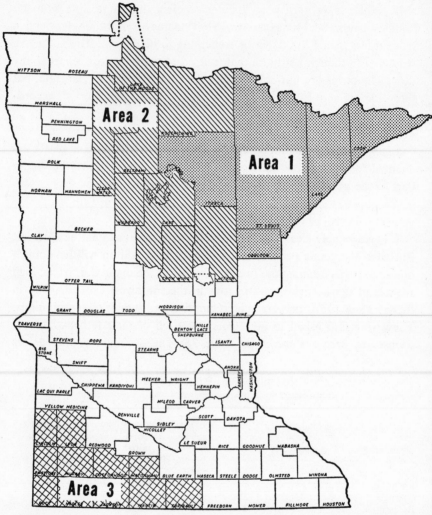

Figure 14. Areas Used in Minnesota High School and Farm Operator
Studies, 1956 (only areas 1 and 2 actually included)

from parental occupations, if their desires are fulfilled, is clear from these
figures. Even though area 3 is predominantly agricultural and one of
the best farming sections of the state — and the country — nearly as large
a proportion of students desire professional careers there as in the northeast. It is understandable that the percentage selecting agriculture would
be higher in area 3 than in the other two areas, but even so, only a tenth

140

Table 34. Occupational Choices of Town and Open-Country Senior High School Boys in Northeastern and Southwestern Minnesota, 1956

Occupational Choice	Town		Open-Country	
	NE	SW	NE	SW
Professional	45.7%	29.4%	26.8%	26.7%
Farming	0.4	7.1	9.3	48.9
Proprietorial, managerial, clerical, and kindred....	20.2	15.3	10.9	2.2
Skilled and semi-skilled..	18.0	24.7	29.6	13.3
Laborer	1.2	0.0	2.3	2.2
No answer or don't know	14.5	23.5	21.0	6.7

of the total made this choice. This is in spite of the fact that 34 per cent of all students, both boys and girls, were children of farmers, compared with the smaller percentages in areas 1 and 2.

Of course, girls and boys differ in their occupational aspirations. Whether the students live in towns or in the open country also makes a difference. The occupational choices of town and open-country boys in the southwest and northeast are shown in Table 34.

The choice of a professional career looms large in all areas, but it is not so popular as farming in the southwest. A goodly proportion of all classes of boys are thinking seriously of skilled and semi-skilled occupations, with the town boys of the southwest ranking highest. When the proprietorial, managerial, clerical, and kindred occupations are grouped, the proportion of all boys choosing these runs rather high, but mainly the town boys of both regions and the open-country residents of the northeast are involved. In the southwest the open-country boys are less interested in this occupational group.

The analysis of these data revealed that about 60 per cent of the boys in the northeast chose occupations of higher rank (according to the prestige rating of occupations by Alba Edwards of the Bureau of the Census) than those their fathers followed. Another 18.5 per cent chose occupations of the same rank as the fathers, and 14 per cent those not so high.[10] Mainly because so many of the southwestern boys were sons of farmers and so many chose farming, only 41 per cent selected occupations higher than those of their fathers, 40 per cent the same and 11 per cent lower.

[10] See Lowry Nelson and A. Majeed Khan, "What High School Graduates Would Like to Do in Life," *Minnesota Farm and Home Science*, Vol. 14, No. 3 (May 1957), pp. 15, 19.

There was much greater dissatisfaction with the father's occupation on the part of the northeastern seniors in both town and open country. This was true also of the girls, although the town girls were more dissatisfied than those in the open country in both regions.

It is quite clear that the northeastern boys, as well as girls, see their futures in occupations outside farming, and the largest group is looking toward the professions. In southwestern Minnesota, where farming opportunities are more promising and more likely available, agriculture is preferred by nearly half of the total.

The blue-collar occupations (skilled and semi-skilled) ran second among the choices, the heavy preference being for professional and other white-collar careers.

Occupational aspirations of the sons of farmers. Among the high school seniors were 175 boys who were sons of farmers in the northeast and 41 in the southwest. Half of the latter and only 11 per cent of the former chose agriculture. The next most frequently mentioned occupation for both areas was "professional." Skilled work, including such jobs as machinist and carpenter, was mentioned by about as many farm boys of the northeast as mentioned professions. Also 28 northeastern boys voted for semi-skilled occupations, including 10 who expected to make the army or navy a career. But 39 of the northeasterners did not answer the question, compared with only 2 of the southwesterners. This betokens a very large uncertainty on the part of the sons of Cutover farmers.[11]

Of all students in the survey, 44 percent expected they would have to move in order to realize their occupational aspirations. Another 14 per cent did not answer or said they did not know. The proportions who expected to move were considerably higher in the predominant farming areas (southwest and area 2 of the northeast) than in the more industrialized section (area 1).

The young people of the Cutover, insofar as high school seniors of this study can speak for them, are looking ahead to occupations considerably higher in status and income than those of their fathers. But in order to reach their goal as professionals, it will be necessary for them to have college and perhaps postgraduate training, depending on the profession. This will require money, which may or may not be forthcoming. In short, these choices represented their hopes and aspirations at the time. There

[11] See A. Majeed Khan, "Aspirations of Northeastern Minnesota Farm Boys, 1956," M.A. thesis, University of Minnesota, 1956.

may be many disappointments and frustrations ahead. Yet it is clear and important that their aims are high. It is important for the Cutover as well as for the state as a whole that the achievement of their high aspirations be facilitated in every way possible.

The vocational experience of past graduates. During the summer of 1958 questionnaires were sent to 1948, 1950, 1952, 1954, and 1956 graduates of six high schools, four in the northeast and two in the southwest. Of the 1,168 graduates, addresses were obtained for and questionnaires sent to 1,058. Of these 739 or 72 per cent were returned. Partial information on another 72 was obtained from secondary sources. The purpose of this survey was to ascertain what had actually been the experience of high school graduates from these areas in the past, as regards both geographic and occupational mobility.

The experience of these graduates reveals the unhappy fact that fewer than one in ten of the men had consistently held jobs at the level of their aspiration or higher, and only one in three had at any time held a job equal to the level of his aspiration at the time of graduation. These aspirations have undergone changes in over half of the group. Only 2 per cent now find themselves in jobs as high on the prestige ladder as they had hoped.

As was true for the 1956 seniors, these graduates aspired in large numbers to professional careers — about a third in both northeast and southwest. The data reveal a strong tendency for the men to aspire to their fathers' occupations. However, the majority have not achieved their objectives, although there is still time for them, especially the recent graduates, to do so. Most of them persist in their original choice.

Migration. A larger proportion of the graduates from the northeast than from the southwest are still in the town or county in which the high school from which they graduated is located. In the southwest, 43 per cent are still in the home county, compared with 53 per cent for the Cutover. Another 6 per cent of the northeasterners are still in the area, bringing the total within the area to 59 per cent. The comparable figure for the southwest is 45 per cent. The reason for this difference is undoubtedly the greater availability of nonfarm jobs in the Cutover. By contrast, the southwest is predominantly agricultural, farming simply cannot absorb all the children reared on farms, and there are comparatively few nonfarm jobs.

Migration out of the area is therefore heavier among the high school graduates of the southwest. However, they do not as a rule move far. More of them than is true of those of the northeast are found within the state, or within the region of which Minnesota is a part — the west north central region of the United States. On the other hand, those who do not stay close to home in the Cutover tend to go farther, to states outside the region or to the armed forces. Or as Coller puts it, "those who migrated from the Northeast clustered in short and long distances and those from the Southwest in the intermediate range" as far as their patterns of migration are concerned.[12]

How "Problematical" Is Our Problem Area?

The survey of farm operators supports the data from the United States Census of Agriculture that farm income in these counties is lower than that for other sections of the state. There has been a marked withdrawal from farming, as indicated by the unusual decline in farms. The level of farm living as measured by the usual indices is below the average. Young people — that is, high school seniors — are not aspiring to careers in farming; rather they are hoping for careers in the professions or skilled occupations. The senior boys in the southwestern high schools aspired to careers in farming in about half the cases. The higher income from farming in this area makes it attractive as an occupation. However, for the years sampled, migration from the southwest has been greater than from the northeast, owing to the relative scarcity of occupational alternatives to farming.

Many other debits for the northeast could be listed: the severe climate, the soil characteristics, the lack of markets — especially in area 2; but it is well to look at the credits also. While averages of farm income, values of land and buildings, and of net worth are not high, the fact remains that a large proportion of the operators have demonstrated that they can make a success of farming in the area. In short, it is true in the northeast as elsewhere that good management combined with farms of adequate size, adequately financed, can make money. A third of the operators estimated their net worth at $10,000 or more. Nearly two fifths of the full-time operators were in this category, and nearly 4 per cent of them estimated their net worth at $30,000 or more.

Another asset of this region is the availability of nonfarm employment. For those farmers, especially in area 1, who lack sufficient land or capital to operate full-time as farmers, the off-farm work comes as a happy supplement to the family income. It is significant that the part-time farmers

[12] Richard Walter Coller, "Geographic Mobility of Selected Rural Minnesota Male High School Graduates," unpublished Ph.D. thesis, University of Minnesota, 1959.

had incomes from all sources of more than twice that of the median income of the full-time farmers. However, the net worth of the latter was considerably above that of the former.

These operators are people with agricultural background. They are not towndwellers who are inexperienced in farming. Moreover, in general they have been in the area a long time, the majority being natives. They recognize that there are problems, and they enumerated a long list of them for the interviewers, but they are optimistic about overcoming at least some of them. There certainly is no sign of unrest sufficient to make them leave. All but a small proportion expect to stay.

While many young people aspire to careers that would require their migrating from the area, the comparative study of past graduates from southwest and northeast reveals that a larger proportion of those from the Cutover are still in the area. Migration has not been as great proportionally as from the southwest. It is quite clear that though many of the seniors in the various years have been compelled to accept more modest occupational goals than those they had at their high school commencements, they still markedly retain their original objectives, even after several years out of high school. The Cutover group has been able to find jobs as skilled tradesmen, or have been trained as teachers without leaving the area.

Institutionally, the Cutover is by no means impoverished. Its schools are among the best in the state, and the proportion of its children attending is high, even at the high school level, where it is higher than in most of the other areas. Moreover, there are opportunities for college education within the area. The University of Minnesota Duluth and the State College at Bemidji provide four years of college for those who wish it and can afford it. They may prepare for careers in teaching and other fields, or qualify for graduate training in law, medicine, engineering, and the like. There is also the School of Agriculture and Experiment Station at Grand Rapids.

State and federal agricultural services are all available in the area. These include the Agriculture Extension Service, the Farmers' Home Administration, the Soil Conservation Service, the Agricultural Conservation Program, State and National Forest Services, the State Conservation Department, and the special Iron Range Rehabilitation Service. Since 1956, additional agricultural agents have been provided through the federal Rural Development Program for low-income areas. There is no lack of services in this area. There would seem to be no reason why any farmer who needs and wants help and advice should be without it.

Another item to be mentioned is that the future of the area has been much brightened — at least in the minds of people — by the opening of the St. Lawrence Seaway. It is impossible to predict the importance of this development in the economy of the area and the state, but at least it has raised morale and encouraged optimism about the future. Taconite mining is another recent development which brightens the future prospects, because the high-grade ore is rapidly being depleted.

The general optimism of the people is reflected in the responses of those included in the survey, both young and old. While agriculture is declining in importance, nonfarm industries are increasing. Besides mining and timber use, tourism is rising rapidly and is perhaps as important a resource for the people of the area as any other; its future is unlimited.

Only in its agriculture, on the objective indices of farm income, net worth, farm level of living, and some others, is the Cutover a problem area. It is by no means among the worst in the United States, but it is still classified as below average. Yet the people are only partly dependent on farming. The area has tremendous nonagricultural resources from which they benefit. By and large, they are not suffering from lack of the necessities of life: some of them are well-to-do. Above all, they like the country and leave it only under duress. They like the lakes and streams and the fishing they provide. They like the woods, and hunting the game which the woods harbors. They even like farming when they can make a go of it. As one farmer said: "I like this country, even when times are hard. I like my neighbors, even like the climate."

It appears that agricultural adjustment is gradually taking place. The number of farms is declining and the average cropland per farm is rising, while the total land in farms has not declined proportionally to the decline in farms: this means that the average size of farm is rising. Part-time farming may increase somewhat, but in general the differences between the attitudes of part-time and full-time farmers are not very great. Most of them have farm background and experience. Many of the part-time operators also belong to labor unions, which divides their interests between farm and nonfarm. Or perhaps it is better to say that this membership tends to integrate them more with town and city occupations. The old differences between town and country appear to be diminishing, and diminishing more rapidly in the Cutover than elsewhere.

x The Future Will Be Different

POPULATION change is the dominant factor in considering the possible future development of life in Minnesota and especially in rural Minnesota. "Change" is used rather than "growth," because not only is simple numerical growth important, but the changes in age, sex, and other aspects within a population are of great importance also. Moreover, while growth is assumed as practically automatic, the wise position to take is that change may possibly result in decline. Indeed, the situation facing the farm population is one of decline for the near future, as it has been for many years in the past. This decline has taken place in spite of the over-all growth in the population of the state and the nation.

Though population prospects loom large in any estimate of the future conditions of life, these prospects are conditioned and influenced by many factors. About these we know very little. Why, for example, does the birth rate in the United States continue high, after a long period of low birth rates? Why, in the atomic age, with so many uncertainties facing the world, are young parents having more children than their parents had? Presumably, many influences are at work, among them the relatively high levels of employment and income which have prevailed since 1940, the removal of the fear of pregnancy and childbirth, and the fact that fatherhood may allow a man deferment from military service.

Whatever the influences which are resulting in the increase in fourth, fifth, sixth, and even seventh births, the facts are that they exist and that the children of today are growing up in larger families than those in which their parents were reared. For the nation as a whole, the Bureau of the Census announced in August, 1958, that the number of children ever born

147

to women ages 15 to 44 was 20 per cent greater in 1957 than in 1950, and that 9.2 per cent of the women ever married in 1957 had 5 or more children compared with 7.4 for the same age group in 1950.[1] The statistics only confirm what everyone knows from observation, if not personal experience: that people are having more babies and having them at younger ages than was true of the previous generation. In fact, the average age at marriage has been declining for many years, and is itself a factor in the rise and maintenance of the birth rate.

The outlook for general population growth in the United States is not to be questioned. When the persons born in the high birth-rate years since 1940 come into the marriage market, the number of children each couple has may decline considerably without bringing about a decline in the total number of babies born in the country. Conditions may arise that will tend to discourage large families and bring down the birth rate, but even with two or three children per couple, the total number may remain high.

These facts give a base for estimating the population for, say, twenty years in the future. The Bureau of the Census has estimated that by 1975 the national population may be somewhere in the neighborhood of 230 million, more or less, depending partly on changes in the social and economic climate. The addition of 60 million more people than there were in 1955 is a prospect which is giving rise to much thought about our ability to provide adequate community organization and institutions. There must be provision for education, for worship, for transportation and communication, and for supplying all the goods and services the nation and the local communities will require.

How is Minnesota to share in this responsibility? What proportion of the vast population will live in the state? What will they be doing to earn their board and keep? How many will be on the farm? How will they distribute themselves among the metropolitan centers, the small towns, and the open country? Whether our estimates are right or wrong only time will show; but plans need to be made for the future, and some estimates must be made, even though they miss the mark. The chances are that past trends are enough of a guide so that future estimates based on them should not be far off.

The most unpredictable, yet most important, determiner of Minnesota's future is its human resources. This seems trite, yet it is so true that it needs repetition. For we tend to be excessively preoccupied with the so-called

[1] *Current Population Reports*, Series p-20, No. 84 (August 8, 1958).

physical resources, without realizing that any deposit in the earth of ores, or coal, or soil, or precious stones; any covering of the earth's surface with plants and forests; or the existence of rivers or mountains, or other natural features — any of these is not really a resource until it has been acted upon by the mind and hand of man. So whether the projected increase of the population is realized or not, whether it is exceeded or not, is only one part of the problem of the future. More important is the quality of the people.

Minnesota, or what is now called by that name, was here long before human beings came. It was here before the Indians came. The forests and streams and lakes were here. Doubtless the wild raspberries, strawberries, blackberries, and all the rest were yielding their annual fruit for the bears and the birds before any human beings lived here. When the Indians came — long, long before the white man — they competed with the birds and bears for the wild fruit, they stalked the game in the forests, and they took the fish from the streams. They lived without agriculture, because they found Nature supplied their need for food and clothing, unaided by human mind and hand. As we said in the beginning, it was European man who introduced agriculture. This reminder of the differences in ways of life of the native inhabitants and the Europeans is intended to emphasize the point that resources are not really resources until they are put to human use. A corollary is that the physical endowments of the earth which became resources depend upon the ingenuity of man to find use for them. The economists use the phrase "level of the arts" to express this unmeasurable and in large part unpredictable factor in the human economy.

Thus it must be said that the future of the communities of Minnesota rests very largely in the hands of its people. But inevitably the different segments of the population will be affected differently by whatever new conditions appear. Developments that may prove favorable to nonagricultural industry may affect adversely the agricultural segment, and vice versa. Although agriculture has advanced in technology in a remarkable fashion, this advance has served to reduce the human labor requirements and therefore the size of the farm population. How far will this reduction go? Is there a limit below which it will not fall? And, if the farm population continues to fall and the size of farms increase, what will be the impact on the rural trade centers?

Minnesota, 1975

Of the possibly sixty million people who will be added to the United States population by 1975, it is estimated that Minnesota will get 716,000.

149

This, the number to be added in the twenty-year period 1955–1975, would mean an annual average increase of 35,800. But from 1950 to 1957, the estimated average annual increase was 44,000. If this rate should be maintained, Minnesota will have 164,000 more people by 1975 than was originally estimated. This would mean a population in 1975 of 3,849,000, or a gain of 22.6 per cent for the two decades. The prediction by the Bureau of the Census is based upon certain assumptions about birth and death rates and migration. Minnesota has been exporting part of its natural increase, or at best receiving few migrants from other states, and it is assumed that what has been true in the past will continue to be true in the future. This assumption, of course, may prove to be quite wrong.

For the United States as a whole the percentage increase is estimated at 38.5. The estimated percentage gains for states near Minnesota are Iowa, 15; Wisconsin, 30.2; North Dakota, 9.5; South Dakota, 13.4; Michigan 45.3. States which are expected to make the greatest gains are those around the eastern, southern, and western boundaries of the country: Arizona, California, Colorado, Connecticut, Delaware, Florida, Maryland, Michigan, Nevada, New Mexico, Oregon, Texas, Utah, Virginia, Washington. All are expected to increase by larger percentages than the national average. States with the expected smallest gains will be those of the Middle West from Texas and Louisiana on the south to the Canadian border, the extreme northeast, and three states of Pennsylvania, West Virginia, and Kentucky.

As is true of all population forecasts, this one can be completely upset by the changes in social, economic, and international conditions. Relaxed or tautened international tensions would have a serious effect on the distribution patterns of the population. Among domestic prospects, the St. Lawrence Seaway, when it gets into full operation, may strongly influence the trend of growth of the Lake States and also of the Upper Midwest in general.

Future farm population. It may be worthwhile to list some of the forces that will affect the future trend of the farm population. First, it is well to review the recent trends. The 1950 Census of Agriculture indicated a decline since 1940 in the number of farms in Minnesota of 18,250. Since the farm population, by enumeration, declined by approximately 100,000, the average decline per farm was a little more than 5 persons. The 1955 Census of Agriculture revealed a further decline in farms — 13,876 between 1950 and 1955, about half of them in the Cutover. If we apply the same figure of 5 persons per farm, we would have a population loss of around 60,000 to 70,000 more.

The definition of a farm is important in classifying the rural farm population. Unfortunately for purposes of charting trends, the federal Bureau of the Census modified the definition for the 1950 Census. The modification was thoroughly justified in the interest of accuracy, but resulted in a "decline" in farms and in farm population which was more apparent than real. The effect of the definition was to eliminate a large number of small tracts which had previously been included as farms.

A farm, according to the census of 1950, was a place of 3 acres or more on which the value of agricultural products, exclusive of home gardens, was $150 or more. Places of less than 3 acres were also classed as farms if the value of products sold amounted to $150 or more.

The Minnesota Department of Agriculture has for many years been making an annual census of farms. Their count and that of the federal census made every five years do not correspond. The state Farm Census is taken annually by the township assessors when they assess property in early May. The federal agricultural census is taken every ten years at the time of the population count, the first week in April. But the mid-decade agricultural census was taken in January. Although the state and federal censuses use three acres as a beginning point in defining a farm, the assessors seem to be somewhat more discriminating than the federal census enumerators. In 1950 the state count of farms was 161,289, while the federal count was 179,101. The state count in 1955 (May) was 153,701; the federal (January) was 165,225. In both the 1950 and 1940 counts, the federal was nearly 20,000 more than the state; the two are considerably closer together in 1955.

We may use the state Farm Census to show the change in number of farms and in farm population from year to year. And, fortunately for our purpose, the state Farm Census began counting the people on farms in 1951, so we have an indication of the trend in both farms and farm people since 1951. The data are given in Table 35.

It is of interest to note that the number of persons per farm has remained rather stable through these years. On the other hand the average persons per farm of those that disappeared, calculated by dividing the decline in the number of people by the decline in the number of farms, has fluctuated somewhat, but on the average was less than that for the remaining farms. It may be that the "lost" farms are those given up by

151

elderly persons in larger proportions, while the active farms are operated by younger and larger families.

The trend in the past quarter century. Since those who attempt to estimate the future trend of population rely chiefly on what the past trend has been, it should be instructive to note the developments in number of farms, farm acreage, and farm population over a period of twenty-five years. For

Table 35. Change in Number of Farms and Farm People in Minnesota by Years, 1951 to 1955

Year	No. Farms	Change	Farm Population	Change	Persons per Farm	Persons per Farm "Lost"
1951	159,681	. .	645,819	. . .	4.04	. . .
1952	157,742	−1,939	636,490	−9,329	4.04	4.8
1953	156,039	−1,703	629,698	−6,792	4.04	4.0
1954	154,277	−1,762	625,453	−4,245	4.05	2.4
1955	153,701	−576	624,071	−1,382	4.06	2.4
1956	150,106	−3,595	606,295	−17,776	4.04	4.9
1957	145,626	−4,480	592,768	−13,527	4.07	3.0
1958	141,143	−4,483	579,765	−13,003	4.11	2.9
Total	. . .	−18,538	.	−66,054	. . .	3.6

Source: State Farm Census for the various years.

this purpose the State Farm Census is used. The following observations may be made in regard to these trends:

1. The number of farms has declined in all areas (Fig. 4) of the state, but there are marked differences among them in the extent of decline.

2. Areas in the southern half of the state showed the least change over the 25-year period.

3. Area 3, in the southwest corner of the state and usually included in the Corn Belt, showed the least change of any of the areas.

4. The greatest changes occur as we move northward. In the Twin Cities area the decline in farms and acreage has come about through suburbanization of the area.

5. Area 8, including the counties of northeastern Minnesota, suffered the heaviest loss of farms, although area 5, which borders it on the south, suffered almost as much.

6. Area 7, the Red River Valley, had a rapid increase in the number of acres in farms, and a modest decline in the number of farms.

Because of this relationship between numbers of farms and numbers of people, we would expect those areas in which there was little decline in farms to show also a small decline in farm population. A breakdown of the data for 1951–1957 by type of farming areas exhibits this relationship: areas which had the least decline in number of farms generally had the

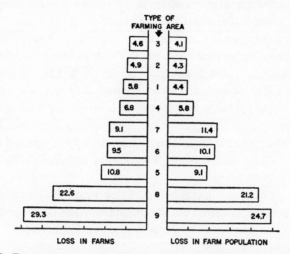

TYPE OF
FARMING AREA

LOSS IN FARMS		LOSS IN FARM POPULATION
4.6	3	4.1
4.9	2	4.3
5.8	1	4.4
6.8	4	5.8
9.1	7	11.4
9.5	6	10.1
10.8	5	9.1
22.6	8	21.2
29.3	9	24.7

Figure 15. Percentage of Decline in Farms and Farm Population by Types of Farming Area, 1951–1957 (Source: State Farm Census; types of farming areas are shown on Figure 4, p. 16)

least loss of farm population, and vice versa (Fig. 15). In short, the heavy losses of farm population occurred in the areas north of the Twin Cities, and of course, in the Twin Cities counties themselves.

Factors Favoring Further Decline

There are both push and pull factors operating to reduce the farm population. The push comes from agricultural technology, the pull from opportunities for working and living in the towns and cities.

The advance of farm technology. The mechanization of agriculture proceeded during the war at a pace which could not have been anticipated. The demand of the military forces for manpower, plus the insatiable demand for workers in the war industries, created a scarcity of labor in agriculture which could only be met by machines. Between 1940 and 1945, even though machinery was hard to come by during the war, the number of tractors increased from 105,000 to 152,500, while the number of horses and mules declined from 160,000 to 146,000. The farm population

153

dropped off by 130,000 during the same period. But the really spectacular increase in tractors and other machines took place after 1945. In the decade following the war, the number of tractors increased to 255,000 or from 118 to 173 tractors per 100 farms.

Tractors are especially numerous in the southern part of the state and in the Red River Valley. In these areas there is an average of around 2 tractors per farm reporting on this item to the census-taker in 1954. Even in the northern and central areas the average is close to 1.5 tractors per farm reporting. It is safe to say that the decade 1945–1955 witnessed a revolution in mechanization. I have reported only tractors, but a similar increase has taken place in other forms of labor-saving machinery — cornpickers, pick-up haybalers, grain combines, milking machines, feed grinders, and so on. Electrification of farms was virtually completed during this decade, and many labor-saving gadgets were installed on farms and in homes.

The pull of nonfarm opportunities. Since 1940, the demand for manpower in nonfarm industries and by the military has been strong and sustained. The war years saw the armed forces built up to over 12 million by 1945. Even with this huge portion of the labor force engaged in war, the civilian population suffered very little from shortages of essential goods and services. It was difficult at that time to see how in peace-time this large manpower "surplus" could be absorbed in the industrial plant. Yet the demobilization was precipitate: to 3 million in 1946, 1.5 million in 1947, and 1.4 million in 1948. Where did they go? Many of them took advantage of the GI Bill to go to college or to take on-the-job or on-the-farm training. Thus, large numbers did not enter the labor force directly. But the point is that opportunities outside of agriculture were sustained, contrary to the expectation of many competent observers.

Partly, of course, full employment was kept up because of the Cold War and the Korean War. By 1952 we had 4.5 million persons in the armed services and the number has stayed at around 3 million since that time. Meantime, the boom conditions in industry have continued partly because of the phenomenal population increase, which demands ever more goods and services, and partly because of the rising income which has enabled families to purchase the goods and services. Thus the pull out of agriculture has been continuous and, in recent years, very strong because of the unfavorable position occupied by farming with respect to the rest of the economy.

154

Factors Favoring Maintenance of Present
Farm Population Numbers

While the factors which push people out of agriculture have been predominant since 1940, it would not be safe to ignore forces which are pulling in the opposite direction. These may at any time achieve dominance and bring about a reversal of the recent trends. For leaving agriculture does not come easily to those who are born and reared on farms and who like farming. Although there are always those for whom farm life is distasteful and who leave for other occupations without a pang, there are also those who want to remain.

The hold of farm life. The desire of people born on the farm to remain there if possible is one of the deterrents to migration out of agriculture. Many people in the United States like farming as an occupation, a fact we tend to overlook. Many young men today want to enter farming, but they lack capital and land. Moreover, there are city people who want to move out onto the land, and there are those who do so by the thousands each year. For many years, the United States Department of Agriculture has made annual estimates of the number of migrants from farms to nonfarm areas and from the nonfarm areas to farms. From 1940 to 1950 it was estimated that 9,300,000 persons left the farm for villages, towns, and cities; but some 4,134,000 moved from villages, towns, and cities to farms.[2] The preference for agricultural life on the part of many persons who grew up on farms, plus many citydwellers' sentimental longing to "return" to the land, must be regarded as important in maintaining farm population. In short, mobility out of agriculture is limited not only by economic opportunities in cities but by emotional attachment to farming as well.

Part-time farming. A trend which is bound to influence upward the farm population is the increasing number of part-time farmers. The upward trend may reflect either of two possibilities. Farm operators who might otherwise have been compelled to leave farming have been able to remain in it because of the supplementary income derived from off-farm work. On the other hand, people regularly employed in urban industry may have acquired small tracts — large enough to be designated farms by the census-taker — on which to live and produce additional income.

The proportion of Minnesota's farm operators who did any work off their farms rose from 20 per cent in 1940 to 35 per cent in 1955. Those

[2] "Farm Population Estimates, January 1949," mimeographed release, Bureau of Agricultural Economics, Washington, D.C., June, 1949.

155

who worked one hundred days or more off their farms rose from 6.7 per cent to 14.9 per cent in the same period; that is, it more than doubled.

The growth of the U.S. and world population. Another obstacle to the continued decline of the farm population is the rapid increase in the non-farm population. The United States alone is adding over three million per year, and the addition to the world population is around forty-seven million. The addition of three million persons to the nonfarm population of the United States is not enough to consume the additional food and fiber the farms are producing, but it is certainly an item to be listed along with others as contributing in the long run to the maintenance of the size of the farm population. It is true that for many years the annual percentage increase in agricultural productivity has been greater than the percentage increase in population. This may also be true in the future; then again it may not. Nothing now in sight indicates a slowing in the rate of productivity increase, but in this matter as in other human affairs, changes can happen quickly and unexpectedly. As of now we should be wary about the prediction so freely made in the past that the increase in population would take care of the agricultural surpluses.[3]

The predicted additional United States population of sixty million by 1975 is a lot of people to feed and clothe. It is important to remember also that not all foods are in surplus supply. While there is no likelihood that the farms of the nation will not be able to meet the needs, the fact of the increase must be listed.

The high birth rate of farm people. Another factor is the larger size of farm families. The difference in birth rate between farm and urban people has lessened in recent years, but there is still a slight margin in favor of the farm people. In the 1940's the urban birth rate in Minnesota actually exceeded the rural, but "rural" included towndwellers as well as farm. It is quite likely that if the birth rate of the farm population were reported separately, it would reveal a rate higher than that of the city. In any case, the number of young people who will be seeking careers either in or out of agriculture will be much greater in the coming decades than it has been since 1940. If they are to be employed outside of agriculture, it is obvious that the number of nonagricultural jobs will have to be greatly expanded.

[3] See John D. Black and James T. Bonnen, *A Balanced United States Agriculture in 1965* (Washington, D.C.: National Planning Association, 1956). These authors estimate that with a population of 189 million, consumption will increase 17 per cent by 1965, and production of food will need to be held to 12.5 per cent over 1955 in order for surpluses to be absorbed.

That is to say, the jobs in industry will have to increase more rapidly in the future because of the rapid expansion in the labor force as a result of the extraordinary increase in births since the war. And if at the same time opportunities in agriculture decline during these years the pressure on industry will be greater still.

Industrial slowdowns. It is a well-known fact that any slackening in industrial employment means a build-up in the farm population. This is not primarily because of any back-to-the-farm movement from the cities; it is the result of the damming up of people on farms who would normally migrate to city jobs if they were available. The generation whose memories reach back to the 1930's remember well the painful conditions of many in agriculture whose labor was not needed there but who could not find jobs elsewhere. It so happened that the largest crops of babies in United States history, up to the recent larger numbers since 1940, were born in the early 1920's and came into their late teens in the 1930's. They were surplus — until the war came in 1940. Then they were a blessing. They went into the armed forces by the millions, and still there were sufficient to man the industries of war. As pointed out earlier, there has been a continued demand for their labor since the war. In the years now rapidly approaching, the multitudes born in high birth-rate years from 1940 on will be joining the labor force. We hope there will be jobs for all of them, and certainly nobody is much concerned about the prospect at this writing. Everyone is optimistic —just as optimistic as the generation of the 1920's and the Great Boom.

A few people, mostly labor leaders, are worried about *automation.* This is a spectacular development because it does away with so many human agents in the production of goods and services. Will it reduce the over-all demand for labor? Some say yes, some no. The answer will be unfolded only with time. But it must be borne in mind that the numbers of persons on farms at any time in a highly industrialized nation is in large part a function of the state of industrial employment. If there is a sustained demand for this rapidly increasing supply of workers, the streams of migrants from agriculture will continue. If the industrial machine falters, the streams will slow down or stop. People may be idle on the farm, or at best partially employed, but they will choose what security the farm affords rather than flee to the uncertainties of the city.

So we must consider the absorbing power of industry as a factor which may cause a build-up of the farm population through decline in demand

157

for labor. It may, of course, continue to operate the other way — that is, to cause a decline in farm people — if full employment is maintained. The Bureau of the Census has reported an estimate of the United States farm population for 1958 somewhat larger than that for 1957, an increase which doubtless reflects the impact of the recession.

War or peace. Another influence on the labor force is the possibility of peace. In reality, the country has been on a war footing ever since 1940. If peace should break out, enabling us to dispense with a large part of the armed forces and discontinue the large production of planes, ships, and guns, we would face a situation in which the competition for a place on the land would be keen indeed. Here again, we have a great uncertainty. If within the next twenty years we could attain a condition of world peace with attendant security, the problem of using the vast labor force in industry would be of a greater magnitude than that of the present.

Shortening the work-week. One way in which the displacement of human labor by machines may be partly offset is by reducing the hours of work without reducing the rates of pay. The theory is that the machines should increase the productivity of the human agent, which it does, and therefore that the human agent is able to work fewer hours to achieve the same output. While the theory has been applied largely in the nonagricultural sector, agriculture has also felt its impact. Hired men are reluctant to work more than an eight-hour day without overtime pay. In the past farmers have scoffed at the idea of limiting the hours of farm work, but the time may be approaching when they will decide that they should share — along with city workers — the benefits of the machine age: more leisure, vacation time, travel, and the like.

On the average, the trend toward fewer hours of work per man-year in farming has been downward in the United States in recent years, and it seems logical to expect a continuation of the trend. This being the case, reduction in hours of work must be classed as a factor maintaining the farm population numbers, since the available work would be shared among more workers.

Small versus big farming. Bigness in farming has its limitations. For one thing, not every farmer is competent to manage a large enterprise. Other operators do not care to undertake the additional risks involved in large-scale operations, even though they may have the managerial ability. Most important of all deterrents to bigness is the declining importance of land in the production process. Expansion is now on a vertical rather than horizontal axis for the most part; more capital and labor is applied to the same area of land. Higher-producing strains of crops and livestock, more effective disease and pest control, and the more generous use of fertilizers increase the potential yields per acre to a remarkable degree. Another factor which may prove to be very important in the humid areas of the United States is sprinkler irrigation. This is not a means of countering drought, because it is possible only in years of normal rainfall. What sprinkling makes possible is the application of water at times when plants need it most. Natural rainfall does not always come at the right times, although the annual precipitation may be "normal" or better. To get water to plants when they need it most may vastly increase yields. As one writer observed recently, "With farm prices depressed and costs increasing the farmer must seek methods whereby he can produce more with less acreage, less labor costs and high utilization of capital equipment."

Public policies. Now that the government enters directly into influencing prices and markets for products of the farms, public policies may be expected to have a bearing on the number of people on farms. For example, insofar as these policies tend to sustain prices arbitrarily and thus reduce competition, no doubt people may be kept in agriculture who might otherwise be forced out. On the other hand, developing new and expanded markets for our products abroad may make possible the employment of more human resources and capital in farming. Moreover, limits on government payments to an individual farmer have been set and there has been agitation during periods of agricultural distress to set a limit on the amount of land one man might own. Such a limit now exists as far as federal reclamation projects are concerned, in that no one person may obtain water for irrigating more than 160 acres. Limitations on acreage are unlikely unless serious distress should come to the whole economy; and a general depression is no longer considered probable. However, there may be legislation to preserve the family farm which would, by direct methods (taxation, limitation of benefit payments, and the like), penalize bigness in farming.

How public agricultural policies can bring about the withdrawal of people from farming is well illustrated by the effect of the Soil Bank. For example, in Roseau County, Minnesota, it is reported in 1959 that a third of the farms have been "banked" and thus taken out of active production; a total of 735 whole farms and many other parts of farms have been put into the Soil Bank for periods of up to ten years. Many of the owners remain on the farm and commute to nonfarm employment, or simply do odd

159

jobs as they become available. Others move away to be nearer their jobs. This is no doubt a major reason for the heavy decline of farms in late years shown in Table 35.[4]

What conclusion may be drawn from these considerations? I would hazard the guess, admittedly with an element of hope, that the numbers of people living on farms will not go much below those of the late 1950's. While the number of large farms may continue to increase, this trend will be largely offset by the growth of small farms for part-time farming. The "hope" part of my guess is that internationally we will arrive within the next quarter century at a stage of less fear and tension, which will make possible reducing the expenditures for defense. This, along with the immense rise in numbers in the labor force, will produce problems of employment which may well drive more people to, or keep them in, agriculture.

What about the Small Towns?

I have already spoken of the population trend of the small places in Minnesota — a trend which is somewhat downward. This is a national trend as well. The metropolitan centers, on the other hand, are growing rapidly. Estimates of population increase by areas since 1950 show that well over ninety per cent of the increase has been in the metropolitan areas. But already these great centers are suffering from numerous problems: transportation, water supply, sewage disposal, and the like. For the most part there are no metropolitan central planning agencies, so that many governments are being set up as the suburbs grow which are trying to meet local problems actually soluble only by central planning and action.

In the face of this hectic and anarchic situation, the inevitable question is Why not try to encourage more people to live in the smaller places? The answer involves the larger question of jobs for people in the smaller places. This in turn leads to the question of getting industries to the smaller places, because with farm population declining, the towns which depend on dispensing goods and services to rural people face a declining market.

Though some national trends favor the decentralization of manufacturing — as a means of utilizing the rural labor supply and as a measure

[4] Russel Asleson, "Soil Bank Aid to Farmers Brings Little Cheer to Towns," *Minneapolis Sunday Tribune*, May 23, 1959. The impact on the small trade centers is discussed at length. Obviously with one third of the farms idle, there is not the demand for new farm machinery or repair parts, for gasoline, fertilizer, prepared feeds, and all other farm supplies. Banks feel the pinch in lowered volume of credit required.

against destruction by bombs — the extent of such decentralization has not been impressive. The main reason for the resistance to decentralization is that places like Detroit and other centers of specialized manufacture have already attracted and trained a pool of skilled workers, workers who would be reluctant to move to other localities. The mobility of industry is related to the mobility of labor.

Still, the fact that industries *do* move is manifest in the vast scale of industrialization in the southern states in recent years. The same can be said of the phenomenal rise of industries in the West, and in the many industrial plants established in smaller places throughout the Middle West, including Minnesota. Industries can be and are being attracted to the smaller places.

But this industrialization needs to be accelerated if the trend to metropolitanism is to be counteracted. In this battle with the giants, the small ones must, like David, use all the ingenuity they can muster. They need to organize and campaign for job-making enterprises. Some of the towns have people with ideas but no capital, as the Inventors Shows at Redwood Falls in 1958 and 1959 demonstrated. But capital is usually forthcoming for the exploitation of new ideas, once the ideas are demonstrated to be useful and practical. If local communities make surveys of their human and physical resources, they are then in a better position to plan for the use of those resources. This is the first responsibility of the leaders of the local community.

If jobs are made available in the local centers, then more people living on farms are able to continue to live in the adjoining open country. Actually, this kind of life is not something for the future; thousands of farm families and other open-country residents are living it today. For while the pace of small-town industrial growth is slow, it is going on. The establishment of the branch factory of the International Business Machines Corporation at Rochester in 1957 is one of the dramatic evidences of this development. Well over a hundred of the more than eight hundred incorporated places in Minnesota have organizations working more or less effectively for industrial growth.

In conclusion, we can say that as of 1960 smaller communities are not competing successfully with the metropolitan areas for the state's increments of population, although the ideal situation for the future of the local community would be to have at least as rapid a rate of industrialization there as in the large centers. As is true nationally, Minnesota's growth is largely in the metropolitan areas, especially that of the Twin Cities, which includes Anoka, Dakota, Hennepin, and Ramsey Counties. Suburbs are springing up to house the workers who serve the expanding industrial complex. Thus, freeways are being projected which will be built at enormous cost to enable these workers to get to their jobs in the centers. Perhaps with more statewide planning, new industries might be encouraged to locate in the smaller places, thus enabling workers who would otherwise move to the metropolis to remain in their home towns.

There is much to be said for the smaller towns as places to live. Even the open country is presently being invaded by many who work in towns and cities. The supposed advantages of living in a city have been largely nullified by rapid transportation. Almost every farmer in Minnesota might be regarded as a suburbanite because he is within a few hours of the metropolis. It is no longer necessary to live in a city to enjoy its advantages.

Integration of town and country. This industrialization of the small places tends to bring town and country closer together. When members of farm families are working in town or city, farm people's understanding of the problems of nonfarm people is bound to increase, and the same thing should be expected from the citydwellers with respect to the farmer. But integration has other aspects as well. More and more, as the special schools and churches for farmers disappear, town and country must share the support and maintenance of these and other social institutions. Farm and town are becoming desegregated. Integration is the key word of the future.

I hope that this necessarily brief review of some of the salient features of community life in rural Minnesota may contribute in a small way to an understanding of our rural heritage. I can think of no other part of the world where within a hundred years there has been such a dramatic transition from a wilderness to an urban industrial economy; from a self-sufficing agriculture to the almost incredible productive agriculture of the 1950's. From a mere 6,000 persons in 1850, the population has risen to an estimated 3,418,000 in 1959. From being an exclusively rural state, Minnesota has become a predominantly urban one.

The achievement of this hundred years is the work of immigrants and their descendants. Few states of the Union have received as many different immigrant stocks as Minnesota. Whether they came from the eastern communities of the new nation or from overseas, they were nevertheless immigrants or the children of immigrants. They all in some way or other contributed to the society we know today. Some, indeed, went through terrible ordeals — crises of weather, of insects and other pests — and their attendant privations on the frontier. Others contributed the organizing initiative, managerial ability, and the sheer physical effort which made the railroads and the lumber, mining, milling, and other industries of the state's economy. But they survived the ordeals; and the changes which were part of growth were facilitated. One must agree with T. C. Blegen when he says, "In my own interpretation of the immigrant in American history, the keynote is not ordeal but transition. Immigrant pioneering was not a fixed mode of life. Its characteristic was change. Nothing was fixed. There was a constant interplay of two creative forces — the Old World heritage and the American environment." [5]

Change has brought new problems in its wake. The transitions in farm power, first from the ox to the horse, then to the motor, have compelled drastic changes in the distribution of the population and in the organization of social institutions. The constant introduction into agriculture of new techniques has so increased the production per man that not only are human beings compelled to leave farming, but land is also pushed out of agricultural use. And all this is in the face of the most rapid growth in population we have ever known. Many more mouths could be fed and bodies clothed with the present rate of farm production.

The old isolation of farms and farm communities has been abolished by the revolutions in both transportation and communication. Today no family is so remote geographically that it cannot at a moment's notice be in touch with news from all parts of the world. Farmers are part of the mass society. They are not only tied into the market economy in such a way as to form an inextricable part of it, but they are bound up in the great political community: the world itself. What they do affects others and what others do affects them in ever more direct ways.

The problems of the twentieth century, whether technological or social, are so complex and immediate as to require farmers with extraordinary aptitudes. The new farmer is an educated man alert to these worldwide developments, aware of his own importance as a member of society and of the importance of his local community. He is in charge of a very complicated enterprise valued at, say, $50,000 or more. Of necessity, he will require advanced education not only in technology of agriculture but in the science of society itself.

[5] T. C. Blegen, *Grass Roots History* (Minneapolis: University of Minnesota Press, 1947).

Bibliography, Appendix, and Index

Bibliography

Monographs and Bulletins on Community Life

MOST of the research on community life in Minnesota has been published as articles in journals or released in mimeographed form. To list these by authors and titles would require many pages and would not interest most of the readers of this book. However, the shorter list of the official bulletins of the Minnesota Agricultural Experiment Station (MAES) and of the University of Minnesota as such, will indicate the nature and scope of research, as well as its historical development. For example, the first published survey of a Minnesota community (by Thompson and Warber) is dated 1913. Two others (Warber and Weld, respectively) date from 1915. These must rank among the earliest studies of this kind in the United States.

Alexander, Frank D., and Lowry Nelson. *Rural Social Organization in Goodhue County.* MAES Bulletin 401. 1949.

Davies, Vernon. *Farm Housing Needs.* MAES Bulletin 393. 1947.

Francis, Roy G. *Mathematical Analyses of Birth Order Data for Minnesota.* MAES Technical Bulletin 216. 1955.

Lively, C. E. *Growth and Decline of Farm Trade Centers in Minnesota, 1905–1930.* MAES Bulletin 287. 1932.

McVoy, Edgar C., and Lowry Nelson. *Satisfactions in Living — Farm Versus Village.* MAES Bulletin 370. 1943.

Murchie, R. W., and M. E. Jarchow. *Population Trends in Minnesota.* MAES Bulletin 327. 1936.

Murchie, R. W., and C. R. Wasson. *The Beltrami Island, Minnesota Resettlement Project.* MAES Bulletin 334. 1937.

Nelson, Lowry. *Education of the Farm Population in Minnesota.* MAES Bulletin 358. 1944.

———. *Minnesota's Farm Population Prospects.* MAES Special unnumbered Series on Postwar Agriculture in Minnesota. 1944.

———. *Red Wing Churches during the War.* Minneapolis: University of Minnesota Press. The Community Basis for Postwar Planning, No. 7. 1946.

———. *Farm Retirement in Minnesota.* MAES Bulletin 394. 1947.

———, and Hazel Clampitt. *Population Trends in Minnesota: 1940.* MAES Bulletin 387. 1945.

THE MINNESOTA COMMUNITY

————, Donald Mitchell, and Ernst Jacobson. *Some Problems of Minnesota Rural Youth.* MAES Bulletin 358. 1942.

————, Charles E. Ramsey, and Jacob Toews. *A Century of Population Growth in Minnesota.* MAES Bulletin 423. 1954.

————, and Roy G. Francis. *Rural-Urban Distribution of Hospital Facilities and Physicians in Minnesota.* MAES Bulletin 432. 1955.

Price, H. Bruce, and C. R. Hoffer. *Services of Rural Trade Centers in Distribution of Farm Supplies.* MAES Bulletin 249. 1928.

Ramsey, Charles E., Alan D. Orman, and Lowry Nelson. *Migration in Minnesota: 1940–50.* MAES Bulletin 422. 1954.

Taylor, Lee, Marvin J. Taves, and Gordon Bultena. *Changing Goodhue County, 1946–58.* MAES Sociology of Rural Life Bulletin No. 1. 1958.

Thompson, Carl W., and G. P. Warber. *Social and Economic Survey of a Rural Township in Southern Minnesota.* Published by the University of Minnesota. 1913.

Warber, Gustav P. *Social and Economic Survey of a Community in Northeastern Minnesota.* Bulletin of the University of Minnesota. 1915.

Weld, L. D. H. *Social and Economic Survey of a Community in the Red River Valley.* Published by the University of Minnesota. 1915.

Zimmerman, Carle C. *How Minnesota Farm Family Incomes are Spent.* MAES Bulletin 234. 1927.

————. *Incomes and Expenditures of Village and Town Families in Minnesota.* MAES Bulletin 253. 1929.

————. *Incomes and Expenditures of Minnesota Farm and City Families.* MAES Bulletin 255. 1929.

————. *Farm Trade Centers in Minnesota, 1905–29: A Study in Rural Social Organization.* MAES Bulletin 269. 1930.

————, and John D. Black. *The Marketing Attitudes of Minnesota Farmers.* MAES Technical Bulletin 45. 1926.

————. *How Minnesota Farm Family Incomes are Spent.* MAES Bulletin, 234. 1927.

————. *Family Living on Successful Farms.* MAES Bulletin 240. 1927.

————. *Factors Affecting Expenditures of Farm Family Incomes in Minnesota.* MAES Bulletin 246. 1928.

168

Appendix

POPULATION TABLES

Table A. Number and Percentage of Minnesota Population in Various
Residence Categories, 1850–1950*

Year	Total	Urban	Rural	Rural Nonfarm	Rural Farm
		Number of Population			
1950	2,982,483	1,607,446	1,375,037	568,519	806,518
1940	2,792,300	1,390,098	1,402,202	496,762	905,440
1930	2,563,953	1,257,616	1,306,337	418,288	888,049
1920	2,387,125	1,051,593	1,335,532	442,072	893,460
1910	2,075,708	850,294	1,225,414	...	...
1900	1,751,394	598,100	1,153,294	...	...
1890	1,310,283	443,049	867,234	...	...
1880	780,773	148,758	632,015	...	...
1870	439,706	70,754	368,952	...	...
1860	172,023	16,223	155,800	...	...
1850	6,077	...	6,077	...	...
		Percentage of the Total Population			
1950	...	53.9	46.1	19.1	27.0
1940	...	49.8	50.2	17.8	32.4
1930	...	49.0	51.0	16.3	34.7
1920	...	44.1	55.9	18.5	37.4
1910	...	41.0	59.0	...	...
1900	...	34.1	65.9	...	...
1890	...	33.8	66.2	...	...
1880	...	19.1	80.9	...	...
1870	...	16.1	83.9	...	...
1860	...	9.4	90.6	...	...
1850	...	...	100.0	...	...

* The definition of urban, rural nonfarm, and rural farm are those used in the
1940 and earlier censuses. The rural farm population was enumerated separately for
the first time in 1920.

169

Table B. Minnesota Population by Counties, 1870–1950

County	1950	1940	1930	1920	1910	1900	1890	1880	1870
Aitkin	14,327	17,865	15,009	15,043	10,371	6,743	2,462	366	178
Anoka	35,579	22,443	18,415	15,626	12,493	11,313	9,884	7,108	3,940
Becker	24,836	26,562	22,503	22,851	18,840	14,375	9,401	5,218	308
Beltrami	24,962	26,107	20,707	27,079	19,337	11,030	312	10	80
Benton	15,911	16,106	15,056	14,073	11,615	9,912	6,284	3,012	1,558
Big Stone	9,607	10,447	9,838	9,766	9,367	8,731	5,722	3,688	24
Blue Earth	38,327	36,203	33,847	31,477	29,337	32,263	29,310	22,889	17,302
Brown	25,895	25,544	23,428	22,421	20,134	19,787	15,817	12,018	6,396
Carlton	24,584	24,212	21,232	19,291	17,559	10,017	5,272	1,230	286
Carver	18,155	17,606	16,936	16,946	17,455	17,544	16,532	14,140	11,586
Cass	19,468	20,646	15,591	15,897	11,620	7,777	1,247	486	380
Chippewa ..	16,739	16,927	15,762	15,720	13,458	12,499	8,555	5,408	1,467
Chisago	12,669	13,124	13,189	14,445	13,537	13,248	10,359	7,982	4,358
Clay	30,363	25,337	23,120	21,780	19,640	17,942	11,517	5,887	92
Clearwater	10,204	11,153	9,546	8,569	6,870	....	....	....	....
Cook	2,900	3,030	2,435	1,841	1,336	810	98	65	....
Cottonwood	15,763	16,143	14,782	14,570	12,651	12,069	7,412	5,533	534
Crow Wing	30,875	30,226	25,627	24,566	16,861	14,250	8,852	2,319	200
Dakota	49,019	39,660	34,592	28,967	25,171	21,733	20,240	17,391	16,312
Dodge	12,624	12,931	12,127	12,552	12,094	13,340	10,864	11,344	8,598
Douglas	21,304	20,369	18,813	19,039	17,669	17,964	14,606	9,130	4,239
Faribault ..	23,879	23,941	21,642	20,998	19,949	22,055	16,708	13,016	9,940
Fillmore	24,465	25,830	24,748	25,330	25,680	28,238	25,966	26,162	24,887
Freeborn ..	24,517	31,780	28,741	24,692	22,282	21,838	17,962	16,069	10,578
Goodhue ..	32,118	31,564	31,317	30,799	31,637	31,137	28,807	29,651	22,618
Grant	9,542	9,828	9,558	9,788	9,114	8,935	6,875	3,004	340
Hennepin ..	676,579	568,899	517,785	415,419	333,480	228,340	185,294	67,013	31,566
Houston	14,435	41,735	13,845	14,013	14,297	15,400	14,653	16,332	14,936
Hubbard ..	11,085	11,085	9,596	10,136	9,831	6,578	1,412	....	....
Isanti	12,123	12,950	12,081	13,278	12,615	11,675	7,607	5,063	2,035
Itasca	33,321	32,996	27,224	23,876	17,208	4,573	743	124	96
Jackson	16,306	16,805	15,863	15,955	14,491	14,793	8,924	4,806	1,825
Kanabec ..	9,192	9,651	8,558	9,086	6,461	4,614	1,579	505	93
Kandiyohi ..	28,644	26,524	23,574	22,060	18,969	18,416	13,997	10,159	1,760
Kittson	9,649	10,717	9,688	10,638	9,669	7,889	5,387	905	64
Koochi-ching	16,910	16,930	14,078	13,520	6,431	....	....	....	....
Lac qui Parle	14,545	15,509	15,398	15,554	15,435	14,289	10,382	4,891	145
Lake	7,781	6,956	7,068	8,251	8,011	4,654	1,299	106	135
Lake of the Woods	4,995	5,975	4,194	....	....	....	....	....	....
Le Sueur ..	19,088	19,227	17,990	17,870	18,609	20,234	19,057	16,103	11,607
Lincoln	10,150	10,797	11,303	11,268	9,874	8,966	5,691	2,945	....
Lyon	22,253	21,569	19,326	18,837	15,722	14,591	9,501	6,257	....
McLeod	22,198	21,380	20,522	20,444	18,691	19,595	17,026	12,342	5,643
Mahnomen	7,059	8,054	6,153	6,197	3,249	....	....	....	....
Marshall ..	16,125	18,364	17,003	19,443	16,338	15,698	9,130	992	....
Martin	25,655	24,656	22,401	21,085	17,518	16,936	9,403	5,249	3,867
Meeker	18,966	19,277	17,914	18,103	17,022	17,753	15,456	11,739	6,090
Mille Lacs	15,165	15,558	14,076	14,180	10,705	8,066	2,845	1,501	1,109
Morrison ..	25,832	27,473	25,442	25,841	24,053	22,891	13,325	5,875	1,681
Mower	42,277	36,113	28,065	25,993	22,640	22,335	18,019	16,799	10,447
Murray	14,801	15,060	13,902	13,631	11,755	11,911	6,692	3,604	209
Nicollet	20,929	18,282	16,550	15,036	14,125	14,774	13,382	12,333	8,362
Nobles	22,435	21,215	18,618	17,917	15,210	14,932	7,958	4,435	117
Norman	12,909	14,746	14,061	14,880	13,446	15,045	10,618	....	....

170

ounty	1950	1940	1930	1920	1910	1900	1890	1880	1870
lmsted	48,228	42,658	35,426	28,014	22,497	23,119	19,806	21,543	19,793
tter Tail..	54,320	53,192	51,006	50,818	46,036	45,375	34,232	18,675	1,968
ennington	12,965	12,913	10,487	12,091	9,376	....	....	....	....
ine	18,223	21,478	20,264	21,117	15,878	11,546	4,052	1,365	648
ipestone....	14,003	13,794	12,238	12,050	9,553	9,264	5,132	2,092	......
olk	35,900	37,734	36,019	37,090	36,001	35,429	30,192	11,433	....
ope	12,862	13,544	13,085	13,631	12,746	12,577	10,032	5,874	2,691
amsey	355,332	309,935	286,721	244,554	223,675	170,554	139,796	45,890	23,085
ed Lake ..	6,806	7,413	6,887	7,263	12,195	....	....	....	....
edwood ..	22,127	22,290	20,620	20,908	18,425	17,261	9,386	5,375	1,829
enville	23,954	24,625	23,645	23,634	23,123	23,693	17,099	10,791	3,219
ice	36,235	32,160	29,974	28,307	25,911	26,080	23,968	22,481	16,083
ock	11,278	10,933	10,962	10,965	10,222	9,668	6,817	3,669	138
oseau	14,505	15,103	12,621	13,305	11,338	6,994	....	....	....
t. Louis....	206,062	206,917	204,596	206,391	163,274	82,932	44,862	4,504	4,561
cott	16,486	15,585	14,116	14,245	14,888	15,147	13,831	13,516	11,042
herburne..	10,661	10,456	9,709	9,651	8,136	7,281	5,908	3,855	2,050
ibley	15,816	16,625	15,865	15,635	15,540	16,862	15,199	10,637	6,725
tearns	70,681	67,200	62,121	55,741	47,733	44,464	34,844	21,956	14,206
teele	21,155	19,749	18,475	18,061	16,146	16,524	13,232	12,460	8,271
tevens	11,106	11,039	10,185	9,778	8,293	8,721	5,251	3,911	174
wift	15,837	15,469	14,735	15,093	12,949	13,503	10,161	7,473	....
odd	25,420	27,438	26,170	26,059	23,407	22,214	12,930	6,133	2,036
raverse ..	8,053	8,283	7,938	7,943	8,049	7,573	4,516	1,507	13
abasha ..	16,878	17,653	17,613	17,919	18,554	18,924	16,972	18,206	15,859
adena	12,806	12,772	10,990	10,699	8,652	7,921	4,053	2,080	6
aseca	14,957	15,186	14,412	14,133	13,466	14,760	13,313	12,385	7,854
ashing-									
n	34,544	26,430	24,753	23,761	26,013	27,808	24,992	19,563	11,809
atonwan..	13,881	13,902	12,802	12,457	11,382	11,496	7,746	5,104	2,426
ilkin	10,567	10,475	9,791	10,187	9,063	8,080	4,346	1,906	295
inona	39,841	37,795	35,144	33,653	33,398	35,686	33,797	27,197	22,319
right	27,716	27,550	27,119	28,685	28,082	29,157	24,164	18,104	9,457
ellow									
ledicine ..	16,279	16,917	16,625	16,550	15,406	14,602	9,854	5,884	....
Total	2,975,523	2,792,300	2,563,953	2,387,125	2,075,708	1,751,394*	1,310,283†	780,773	439,706‡

* The total for 1900 includes population (3,486) of White Earth Indian Reservation, in Becker, Clearwater, and Mahnomen Counties, not returned by counties for that year.
† The total for 1890 includes population (8,457) of Indian reservations specially enumerated but not distributed by counties.
‡ The total for 1870 includes population of Monongalia County (3,161) annexed to Kandiyohi County in 1870. Kittson County name was changed from Pembina in 1878.

Index

Age: and tenancy, 11; composition of population, 24–26, 31, 55
Agriculture: development in Minnesota, 3, 19; in the Cutover, 126–127, 129–139
Aitkin County, 120
Alexander, Frank D., 103n
Anderson, William, 101n, 107n, 110n
Anglo-Americans, 52, 62
Anoka County, 23
Asleson, Russel, 160n
Assimilation: intermarriage as test of, 45; organized religion and, 47–48; propinquity and, 49; differences among groups in desire for, 49–50; immigrant organizations and, 50; of churches, 124. *See also* Ethnic groups
Austin, 24
Ayer, Frederick, 115

Birth rate. *See* Family
Black, John D., 71n, 156n
Blegen, T. C., 17n, 163n
Bohemians, 52, 90
Bonnen, James T., 156n
Bonwell, Mary R., 68n
Bowles, Gladys K., 72n
Buck, Roy C., 112n
Bultena, Gordon, 87n

Carver County, 63
Catholic Church. *See* Roman Catholic Church
Chapin, F. Stuart, 71n

Children, 56, 65–69, 139–144. *See also* Family
Chinese, 41
Chippewa National Forest, 127
Chisago County, 24
Churches: early history, 114–116; number, 116–117; denominational diversity, 117; geographic distribution, 117–120; rate of growth of membership, 120; comparison of rural and urban growth rates, 121; demographic explanation for growth of, 121–123; mergers and cooperation among, 124–125
Cities, 20–22
Clampitt, Hazel, 18n
Clay County, 45, 53
Coller, Richard W., 144n
Consolidated schools, adjustment to, 68
Conveniences, 72–76
Cook County, 120, 127
Copp, James H., 61n
Corner, Faye E., 5n
County, 101–105
Cutover: farm tenancy in, 11; as population "sponge," 24; in-group marriage in, 45; importance, 126–127; timber and mining development in, 127–128; ethnic groups in early settlement of, 128; trends in the number of farms of, 128; economic status among part- and full-time farmers of, 131–133; social characteristics of farm operators in, 133–136; farmers' problems in, 136–138; oc-

172

cupational aspirations of seniors in high schools of, 139–143; vocational experience of former high school graduates of, 143–144; problems and prospects of, 144–146

Czechs, 43

Dakota County, 24, 103
Danes, 39, 40
Davies, Vernon, 77n
Death rate, 59
Deininger, Marian, 52n
Detroit Lakes, 67
Divorce, 56, 64–65
Dodge County, 49
Donohue, George A., 14n, 15n
Du Lhut, 4
Duluth, 21–22, 126, 131
Dutch, 52

East, Wendell L., 5n
Education: effect on migration, 34; pioneer period of, 84–85; constitutional requirement to provide, 82–86; rural school district, 86–87; school attendance and level of, 88–89; reasons for Minnesota's low rank in rural, 89–98
Electricity. See Conveniences
Ethnic groups: origins, 39–41; Negroes, Indians, Orientals, 41–42; use of Old World languages, 42–45; in-group marriage among, 45–48; assimilation of, 47, 49–52; different attitudes toward school attendance, 89–98

Family: composition, 56–58; size, 58, 60–62; head of, 60–61; marriage patterns and, 62–63; ethnic and religious factors in, 63–64; effect of marriage and divorce on, 64–65; children's attitudes toward, 65–66; personality adjustment of children in, 66–69
Farm population: recent decline in size of, 151–153; types of farming areas and changes in, 153; technology as a factor in decline of, 153–154; effect of nonfarm job opportunities on, 154; part-time farming related to future size of, 155; effect of world population growth on, 156; high birth rate in, 156–157; effect of industrial recession on, 157–158; effect of war or peace on future size of, 158; effect of public policies on, 159–160

Farms: number and size of since 1850, 8, 100; 1950–1954, 9; migration from, 26–27; ownership, 56, 131; in Cutover, 130–139
Fillmore County, 49
Finns, 39, 40, 46, 49, 96
Fort Snelling, 5
French, 43
Frost, Robert, 17

Galpin, Charles J., 100n
Germans, 39, 40, 46, 48, 51, 90, 93, 96, 115
Goodhue County, 49, 87, 102–105, 112
Government: functions of, 99; pattern of settlement's effect on, 100; county, 101–106; town, 106–107; village, 108–109; school district, 109; trends in number of units of, 110; a proposed new unit of, 111–113
Grand Rapids, 67, 68
Groseilliers, Médart Chouart, Sieur de, 4

Hagood, Margaret J., 72n
Hassinger, Edward W., 30n
Hennepin, Louis, 4, 114
Hennepin County, 23, 120
Hiller, E. T., 5n
Holbrook, Stewart H., 127n
Homestead Act (1862), 5, 51, 100
Housing. See Level of living
Houston County, 49

Icelanders, 40
Immigration. See various nationalities
Indians, 5, 41–42, 50, 114
Industry, 160, 161
Intermarriage, 45–48
Irish, 52
Iron mining, 126–127
Isanti County, 73–74

Japanese, 41
Jarchow, Merrill E., 6n, 18n, 85n
Jesness, Oscar B., 128n

Khan, A. Majeed, 141n, 142n
Kirkpatrick, E. L., 71n

Labor unions, 135, 146
Lake County, 23, 127
Land settlement: Pre-emption Act, 6, 100; Homestead Act, 6, 100; patterns of, 100
Land tenure: trends in, 9–11; social sig-

nificance of, 11–12; age of operator and, 12; part-time farming and, 15
Language, 42–45, 124
Level of living: measures of, 72; satisfaction with, 72–75; housing aspects of, 75–79; nonmaterial aspects of, 79–82
Lutheran Church, 52, 62, 90, 96, 115, 116, 124

McClusky, Howard Y., 63n
MacLeish, Archibald, 4n
McVoy, Edgar C., 74n
Mangus, A. R., 67n
Marquette, Jacques, 4
Marriage, 54–55, 62–65. *See also* Intermarriage
Marshall, Douglas, 35n, 52n, 62n, 91n, 139n
Migration: present, 28–31; from Cutover, 143–144
Minneapolis. *See* Twin Cities
Mitchell, Donald, 63n
Mixed marriage. *See* Intermarriage
Moltke, 96
Mora, 65
Morrill Act (*1862*), 6
Morris Act (*1902*), 127
Mount, Robert R., 72n
Murchie, R. W., 18n

Negroes, 41–42
Nelson, Lowry, 15n, 18n, 35n, 45n, 66n, 74n, 76n, 89n, 103n, 139n, 141n
Nicolet, Jean, 4
Nobles County, 12
Nodland, Truman R., 16n
Northeastern Minnesota. *See* Cutover
Northwestern Minnesota, 46–47
Norwegians, 39, 40, 49, 51–52, 62, 95–96, 124
Nowell, Reynolds I., 128n
Nye, Ivan, 67n

Orientals, 41–42
Orman, Allan D., 18n

Part-time farming, 12–15, 136, 146, 155–156
Peterson, Milo, 35n, 91n, 139n
Pierz, Francis X., 115
Pipestone, 67
Poles, 46, 52, 90
Pond, George A., 16n
Population: growth of since *1850*, 19–23;

urban increase, 19–21; rural decline, 22–23; by types of farming areas, 23–24; age composition of, 24–26; sex composition of, 26; migration of, 27–28; community problems and migration of, 28–30; change of by size of place, 29–30; selectivity in migration of, 30–38; birth and death rates in, 58–60; prospects for future growth of, 147–150
Pre-emption Act (*1841*), 6, 100
Propinquity and intermarriage, 49
Protestants, 48, 115, 116, 117, 120–121, 124
Public domain, disposal of, 6–7

Ramsey, Charles E., 18n, 66n
Ramsey County, 23, 120
REA, 76
Red River Valley, 16, 21, 49, 152, 154
Red Wing, 24
Religion and assimilation, 47–48
Rochester, 24, 161
Roman Catholics, 47, 62, 90, 93–95, 115
Roseau County, 159
Rosewood, 95–96
Rundquist, Edward A., 66n
Rural schools, 86–87, 89–98
Russians, 51

St. Lawrence Seaway, 126, 146, 150
St. Louis County, 128
St. Martin, 93–95
St. Paul. *See* Twin Cities
School district, 86–87, 109
Schools: pioneer, 85–86; in Cutover, 135. *See also* Morrill Act, Rural schools, School district
Scott County, 63
Settlement, history of, 5–7
Sewell, William H., 71n
Sex composition: of population, 26, 33, 56, 122; of migrants, 37
Sibley County, 96
Sletto, Raymond F., 66n
Small towns: trends in population of, 29; factors in growth and decline of, 30; future of, 160–162
Southeastern Minnesota, 16, 92
Southwestern Minnesota, 12, 13, 15, 16, 49, 92, 142, 152
Special districts, 109–110
Stearns County, 115
Superior National Forest, 127
Swedes, 39, 40, 52, 62

174

Taves, Marvin J., 67n, 68n, 75n, 87n
Taylor, Lee, 87n
Technology, 37, 153–154
Telephones. *See* Conveniences
Tenancy, farm, 10–12
Thief River Falls, 67
Timber, 127. *See also* Cutover
Toews, Jacob, 18n
Town, 106–107
Trade area as new governmental unit, 111–113
Twin Cities, 13, 21–22, 24, 34–35
Types of farming areas: in Minnesota, 15–17; description of, 16; natural and cultural features of, 17; change in population of, 23; distribution of population and church membership by, 119; the Cutover as one, 126–146; recent farm population changes in, 153

Urban growth, 20–22

Village, incorporated, 108

Waseca, 67
Washington County, 23, 24
Wawina, 96
Wilson, Warren H., 85n
Winona, 24
Wright County, 45, 53

Zander, Alvin, 63n
Zimmerman, Carle C., 71n, 75n, 76n